CW01024985

The Buckley Potteries

Recent Research and Excavation

Nigel W. Jones

With contributions by

Peter Davey, Leigh Dodd, Richard Hankinson,
Bob Silvester and Sophie Watson

ARCHAEOPRESS ARCHAEOLOGY

ARCHAEOPRESS PUBLISHING LTD
Summertown Pavilion
18-24 Middle Way
Summertown
Oxford OX2 7LG

www.archaeopress.com

ISBN 978-1-78969-222-8
ISBN 978-1-78969-223-5 (e-Pdf)

© the individual authors and Archaeopress 2019

Cover: The base of the beehive kiln at Lewis's Pottery (Site 5) during excavations in 2000

Back cover: Workers at Hayes Pottery, Buckley c. 1910. Courtesy of Flintshire Record Office.

Printed in England by Holywell Press, Oxford

This book is available direct from Archaeopress or from our website www.archaeopress.com

Contents

List of Figures and Tables

Acknowledgements

Particular thanks are due to Dr Peter Davey and Christine Longworth for their invaluable assistance with the project as a whole, Will Davies, Cadw Regional Inspector of Ancient Monuments, and Paul Belford for his assistance in editing. Thanks are also due to members of the Buckley Society, particularly Paul Davies and Carol Shone, and the staff of Flintshire Record Office.

The writers would also like to thank Paul Brockley, Flintshire Council, for arranging permission to excavate at Brookhill, which was also facilitated by the work of the following: Matthew Ellis, Senior Species Officer, and Neil Smith, Senior Conservation Officer, Natural Resources Wales; Amanda Davies, Flintshire Council; Mandy Cartwright, Amphibian and Reptile Conservation; and Pip Perry. Pottery drawings are by Sophie Watson, with the exception of those from Taylor's and Lewis's Potteries, which were drawn by Leigh Dodd.

The production of this volume, as well as the assessment and evaluation work undertaken by CPAT, was funded with grant aid from Cadw.

Introduction

Despite Buckley's impressive industrial past, a visit to the town today reveals little evidence to suggest the extent and importance of what were once major regional industries. The remains of brickworks, potteries and collieries are now extremely scarce, the area having seen extensive redevelopment during the last 20 years.

Between 2013 and 2017 the Clwyd-Powys Archaeological Trust (CPAT) conducted an assessment of the Buckley pottery industry, followed by small-scale fieldwork on the site of three of the potteries (Jones 2014; Hankinson and Culshaw 2014; Hankinson 2015; Hankinson and Culshaw 2015; Watson and Culshaw 2015; Hankinson 2017). The results of the project, which has been funded by Cadw, are presented here, together with summary reports on two excavations undertaken by Earthworks Archaeology.

The small town of Buckley, in Flintshire, lies 13km west of Chester and 4km east of Mold (Figure 1). The area surrounding Buckley has been associated with the production of pottery for at least 600 years, from the medieval period to the mid-20th century. The scale and location of pottery manufacture during the Middle Ages and through the Tudor period is poorly known, but by the early 17th century a group of cottage potters had settled around Buckley Mountain where they exploited the suitable supplies of clay, coal and, on Halkyn Mountain, lead. Potteries were often established on encroachments on common land, which can be readily identified in 18th- and 19th-century cartographic sources.

Contemporary accounts are few, although the Buckley potteries were noted by the late 18th-century traveller and writer Thomas Pennant: 'within the lordship are very considerable potteries of coarse earthenware; such as pans, jugs, great pots for butter, plates, dishes, ovens, flower pots, etc. There are fourteen works, which make annually between three and four thousand pounds worth. The ware is mostly exported to Ireland, and the towns on the Welsh coast, particularly to Swansea' (Pennant 1786, 91). Several years later, in 1798, the Reverend Richard Warner provided a fascinating and detailed account of pottery manufacture in Buckley (Warner 1813, 244-7). His introduction to the area states that 'we ascended Buckley hill, in order to visit the large potteries scattered over the face of it; fortunately we met with the master of the works on the spot, who was so good as to conduct us round the manufactury'. Samuel Lewis, in his *Topographical Dictionary of Wales*, also made reference to the industry, although in less detail: 'potteries for the manufacture of coarse earthenwares, and kilns for making fire-bricks and tiles of superior quality, a considerable quantity of which is shipped to Ireland' (Lewis 1833, listed under Coed-Eulo).

It is worth noting here that while Buckley may have been an important supplier of traditional earthenwares, a number of other centres also made a very similar range of products, also based on Coal Measures clays. The most important of these from a north Wales perspective are Stoke-on-Trent, Liverpool/South Lancashire, Whitehaven, and the Glasgow area. Each of these produced black-glazed, red-bodied earthenwares using very similar clays and techniques to those at Buckley. The identification, particularly in archaeological circles, of this style of pottery as 'Buckley Ware' is clearly unreliable and likely to be misleading (Davey and Longworth 2001, 64).

Research by the Buckley Society, the Buckley Clay Industries Research Committee, and others from the mid-1970s onwards had previously identified 19 possible pottery production sites, few of which had been subject to any detailed examination. A recent review of cartographic evidence has increased this number to 31 (Jones 2014), which are listed in the Gazetteer section of this volume, although some are not well located. The overall distribution of potteries is shown in Figure 1, while a basic timeline has been developed which indicates in broad terms their relative life spans (Figure 2).

Evidence from the few excavations, and particularly as a result of work by Jim Bentley and Martin Harrison in the 1970s and 1980s has, however, identified a number of pottery styles and products which are sufficiently different to allow their possible or probable identification when they are found elsewhere.

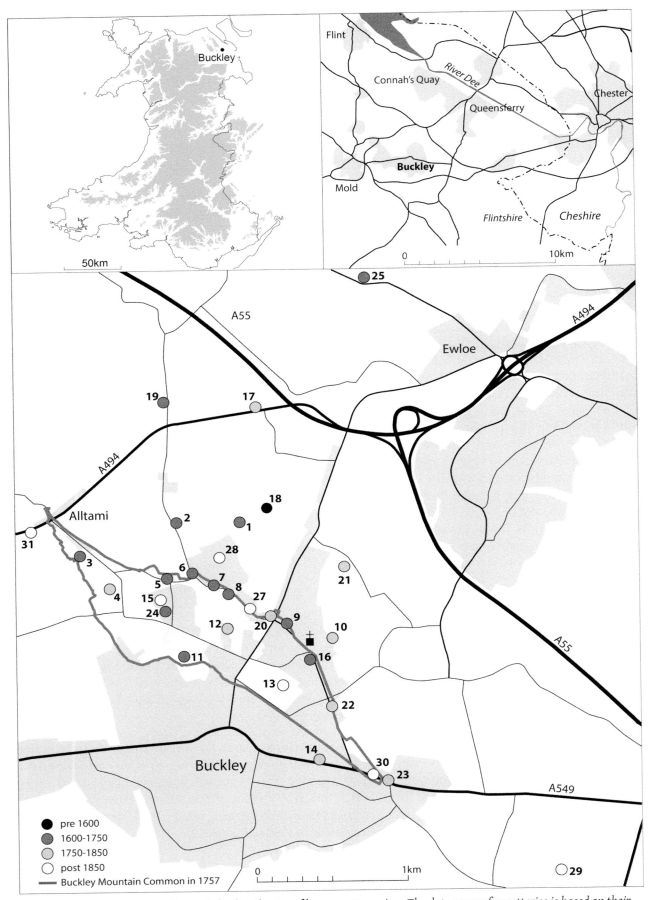

Figure 1 *The location of Buckley and the distribution of known pottery sites. The date ranges for potteries is based on their earliest known date rather than their period of operation.*

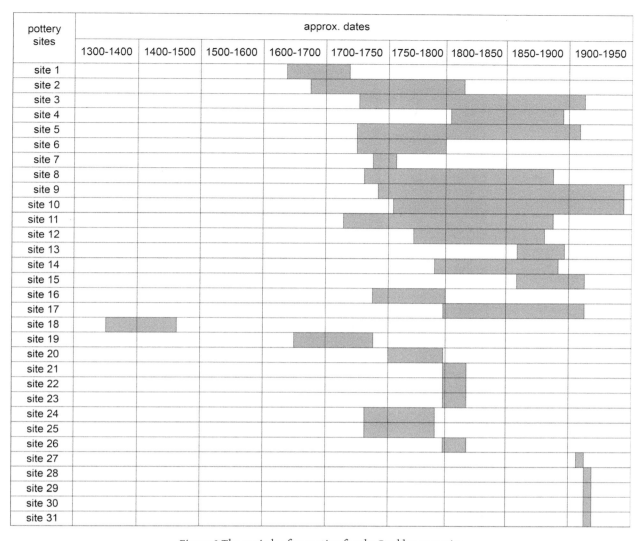

Figure 2 The periods of operation for the Buckley potteries.

Broadly, these comprise the following, though readers are referred to Davey and Longworth 2001 for further detail:

- clay tobacco pipes with the initial TH or Thomas Heyes on the underside of the tailed heel.
- thrown sgraffito ware in a red fabric, all-over yellow slip and lead glaze, with the use of distinctive animal or geometric designs.
- Tripod cooking pots, found in the earliest contexts at Brookhill (Site 1).
- Thrown slipwares with a similar fabric and decoration to the sgraffito vessels.
- Press-moulded slipwares – fragments of moulds and wasters are known from Sites 1 and 2.
- Moulded handles applied to black-glazed and slipware products from Brookhill (Site 1).
- Distinctive thrown forms from Brookhill (Site 1), including large, flared, heavily built beakers, thick-walled pedestal cups or lamps, and trailed slip biconical vessels.
- Mottled wares are not particularly distinctive, but Buckley products are dominated by dishes, many of which were slip-coated before glazing.

The Buckley area has seen considerable new development in the last 20 years, to an extent that significant elements of the pottery industry have already been lost. There are, however, some remarkable survivals, including the site of the Brookhill Pottery (Site 1), which was in operation from *c.* 1640-1720 and was partially excavated by James Bentley, although his work remains unpublished. A substantial archive of finds, site records and related documents – including those derived from the Bentley and Harrison excavations at Brookhill and Pinfold Lane (Site 2) – has been donated to National Museums Liverpool. A smaller collection of material from a number of the sites is held by Flintshire Museums Service.

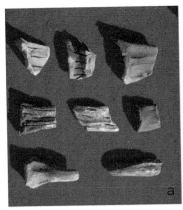

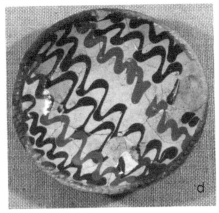

Figure 3 Examples of Buckley wares: a – medieval pottery from Site 18; b and c – sgraffito dish and slipware dish from Brookhill (Site 1); d, e and f – press-moulded dish, trailed slipware dish and black glazed cup from Cotterell's Pottery (Site 2); g – 19th-century brewing jar; h – 19th-century jugs ; i – 19th-century black glazed cup; j – Catherall's stoneware. Photos courtesy of Peter Davey.

Geology of the Buckley Area

Richard Hankinson

The pottery (and brick-making) industry developed in the Buckley area as a result of the availability of suitable raw materials, as well as plentiful fuel in the form of coal. The geology of the locality comprises rocks belonging to the Westphalian (Coal Measures) and Namurian (Millstone Grit) divisions of the Carboniferous period (1994 BGS map of Wales). Within these broad classifications, the main formation exploited at Buckley was the Ruabon Marl, previously known locally as the 'Buckley Fireclay' or 'Buckley Formation', which in this area is around 200m thick and comprises a sequence of mudstones, siltstones and sandstones; occasional thin seams of coal are known elsewhere in the formation. The fireclays outcrop along a major fault, known as the Great Fireclay Fault, as well as along several minor faults. The banding or mottling present in the marl often shows evidence that the layers were seatearths displaying evidence of rootlet penetration and soil formation. Overall, the rocks are associated with the accumulation of alluvial floodplain deposits in the late Westphalian, mostly above the water-table though periodically in anaerobic, waterlogged conditions (Davies *et al.* 2004, 110).

It is significant that the Ruabon Marl formation outcrops at the surface in the Buckley district, where it occurs as a series of fault-bounded inliers, the mudstones of which were those worked for refractory clays (Davies *et al.* 2004, 110). Differential subsidence across faults in the Duckmantian part of the Westphalian led to the formation of block and basin topography, which gave rise to the erosion of higher ground and deposition in the intervening basins (Davies *et al.* 2004, 112), and this, perhaps in part, may explain the restricted extent of the suitable deposits at Buckley.

The material used at Buckley comprised grey, red and purple mudstones and fireclays, worked in two crops, but only the lowest 15m in the Ruabon Marl succession was worked (Davies *et al.* 2004, 166). Historically, acid-resistant goods and refractories were produced using fireclays, but more recently the fireclays were blended with the associated mudstones and sandstones to produce facing bricks and paviours (Davies *et al.* 2004, 166-167). This material, which was extracted from the underlying rocks of the area, was generally used for coarser products such as saggars and bricks.

The pottery on the other hand was made from material derived from near-surface clay deposits, or tills, which were deposited during glaciation. Two sources of glacial material are known, one from north and central Wales and the second from the Irish Sea (Campbell and Hains 1988, 84). The deposition of these near-surface clays would probably also have been dependant on the local topography, and they are therefore highly localised and most probably variable in composition. Local knowledge would have been an important factor in choosing a suitable clay for the particular vessels that were required and it is also possible that the surface clays and underlying marl were mixed when required (P. Davey pers comm.).

The surface soils are fine loamy and clayey soils derived from the underlying rocks and belong to the Brickfield 3 Soil Association (1983 Soil Survey of England and Wales map and legend).

Buckley Potteries and their relationship with Buckley Mountain Common – cartographic evidence

Bob Silvester

The distribution of Buckley potteries (Figure 1) clearly shows a close relationship between the earlier sites and Buckley Mountain Common. This relationship can be elucidated further through map regression analysis. This simple technique adopts a stratigraphic approach, comparing landscape change through time by studying a sequence of maps of the same area. This approach can be generally unpredictable in Wales, largely because of a dearth of larger-scale maps from before the middle of the 18th century. For example, there are at present only seven manuscript maps known for Flintshire from before 1700. Consequently, it is unusual to be able to meaningfully analyse landscape change which took place much before 1750, and in some cases even before the post-1836 tithe survey.

Fortunately, Buckley Mountain fell within the Lordship of Ewloe in the 18th century (and presumably in earlier times), which was mapped – whether in its entirety or in part – on several occasions during the second half of the 18th century. The earliest map dates from 1757, and there is a succession of maps in the Gwysaney archives, of varying usefulness, from then through to the later 19th century. Unfortunately, other estate archives contribute virtually nothing. The Ordnance Survey's first survey drawings were followed rapidly by the tithe surveys after the Commutation Act of 1836, and map analysis ends in the last decades of the 19th century and the beginning of the 20th century, with the large-scale Ordnance Survey plans.

Buckley Mountain – the common

Buckley Mountain had undoubtedly been open common for 'time out of mind', unenclosed, used for grazing and probably providing subsistence materials for the local communities that lived beyond its boundaries. It was not identified on Christopher Saxton's county map published in 1577, nor on the derivative version created by John Speed in 1610, but then neither mapmaker was particularly concerned with naming specific topographical landmarks. William Williams on his 'New Map of the Counties of Denbigh and Flint', usually attributed to 1720-1, named Buckley Mountain, but made no effort to define its outline, unsurprising given the map's small scale.

Figure 4 Buckley Mountain as depicted on the c.1757 map of Ewloe lordship (GW 651). Dark areas represent encroachments and enclosures on the common. Reproduced with the permission of the Gwysaney Estate and the Flintshire Record Office.

The most informative source is the 1757 Lordship of Ewloe map. This is the earliest of the larger-scale maps and particularly clear. The northern perimeter of the common is reasonably easy to distinguish, despite several small and irregular encroachments projecting into the open ground, which clearly were already in existence at the time of the map's creation. The southern boundary is likely to have been formed by the Ewloe Brook (as named on early Ordnance Survey mapping but called the Aber Llanerch Brook in 1757 and the Alltami Brook on late 19th-century maps). This would be consistent with other lowland commons in east Wales. The stream's significance as a boundary was reinforced in the 19th century, by the provision of two boundary stones beside the stream and marked 'P. B. Davis Cooke Esq' according to a traced map of 1860 (GW/748). Other boundary stones in the vicinity of the 'Horse and Jockey' Inn are marked 'E.L.' Today, the boundary east of Hawkesbury Place is rather more regular than in the 18th century, though the alignment has remained broadly the same.

Further to the south-east there are difficulties in distinguishing the precise edge of the common even in the middle of the 18th century. The eastern boundary in the vicinity of Knowl Hill is clearly an artificial division – it separated the Lordship of Ewloe from that of Hawarden. In landscape terms Buckley Mountain will almost certainly have continued into Hawarden lordship but for obvious reasons that continuation is not depicted on the 1757 map, though it can be reconstructed on its northern edge with reasonable certainty from a map of the Hawarden lordship produced in 1733. Its southern edge here is hypothetical because it fell within a third lordship, that of Mold, which is not represented cartographically in the 18th century, and by the time the Ordnance Surveyors moved into the area in 1834, the common edge had retracted to the Knowl Lane crossroads. This apart, the 1757 map provides a reasonably accurate picture of Buckley Mountain, and there is, as yet, no evidence to infer that open ground had formerly extended as far south as Buckley village.

The 1757 map also shows two large pools on the common – Buckley Lake and Bright Lake. Only their approximate locations can be identified, for the former had gone by 1792, the latter between 1834 and 1841.

Buckley Mountain – encroachments and enclosures

The map of 1757 shows encroachments along the length of Buckley Mountain. Some of these can be identified within the overall pattern of enclosures that were subsequently depicted on late 19th-century Ordnance Survey maps, but the location of others is not so clear. For example, the boundary of the encroachment that preceded the later 19th-century Belmont Brickworks cannot be determined with any precision. Similarly, the introduction of a tramroad to serve one of the brickworks resulted in a reconfiguration of the landscape that partially obscured an enclosure immediately south of St Matthew's Church. The segment of land between Aberllanerch Farm and Hawkesbury Place and edged by the Ewloe Brook is considered to be encroachment, though not specifically signalled on any of the historic maps – its field pattern however is suggestive of progressive intakes, of an earlier date than those which were mapped in 1757.

Between 1757 and 1792 the mapped evidence indicates relatively little new enclosure on the common, and where it did occur it took the form of enlargements to existing intakes. The exception could be Hawkesbury Place, which is depicted on the 1792 map in a way that suggests a new encroachment. However, if this was the case it could be inferred that it had formerly extended south of the projected line of Ewloe Brook. The Gwysaney Rentals record 32 encroachments in 1759, with a further two by 1779 and by 1789 this had increased to 62 (Messham 1956, 32).

The fifty years that separated the 1792 lordship map from the Tithe survey saw considerable enclosure of the common - by 1799 over 100 encroachments are listed in the Gwysaney Rentals. The Tithe map is not as accurate as it could have been and in the vicinity of Knowl Lane, in particular, there are mapping errors that cannot be resolved. The final stage in enclosure recognition, up to the Ordnance Survey mapping of 1873/4, reveals a tailing off, of piecemeal enclosure, yet also the increasing encroachment of other industrial operations onto the mountain. It might also be noted here that there was no parliamentary enclosure of Buckley Mountain; it was all done with landowner agreement and perhaps on occasions by the landowner himself.

The Potteries

Cartographic evidence indicates that of the 31 potteries currently known in the Buckley area, 17 were located on or around the edge of Buckley Mountain Common. Of these, nine have their origins in the period 1600 to1750, four between 1750 and 1850, while a further four date from the late 19th and 20th centuries. The mapped evidence is, however, by no means conclusive. Some, such as Sites 5 and 9, were located within enclosures which encroached onto the common, while others, like Sites 6 and 24 lay on the open common itself, and in the case of Sites 3 and 8 the kilns were located on the common, while the buildings were on enclosed land (Messham 1958, 32).

The common, and encroachments onto it, provided an opportunity for the landless class, as well as incomers, to establish potteries with ready access to suitable clay and water. Clay accounts exist in the rentals of the Gwysaney estate from 1759, and from 1783 more detailed records identify the names of potters and the loads of clay they took. For 20 years thereafter about a dozen potters took an average of 600 loads of clay a year, while during the next ten years this increased to almost 1000 loads a year.

In the 18th century, property maps offer the only visual indicators of the potteries. Their representation is likely to be selective, depending on whether the land on which they lay belonged to the commissioning estate and also whether the map itself is sufficiently detailed for the land that it portrayed to be recognised. The 1757 map specifically identifies six potteries (Sites 3, 5, 8, 9, 16 and 24) by using a stylised depiction for the kilns, while in the case of three others (Sites 6, 7 and 11) buildings are depicted which correspond with potteries shown on later mapping, but without any indication of the kilns. The best example of this style of depiction is the pottery established by Jonathan Catherall (Site 8), where three kilns are shown (Figure 5). Of particular interest is the depiction of Site 24, where a single kiln is shown on the common, immediately adjacent to an enclosure in the middle of Buckley Mountain. This is the only evidence for this pottery, which lies close to the later Ewloe or Powell's Pottery (Site 15).

About twenty years later, on one (XI) of a set of Gwysaney maps from around 1780 only two potteries are shown. Both are situated on lanes leading off the north-western side of Buckley Mountain, and neither survived to the end of the 19th century. On another (XII) in the same

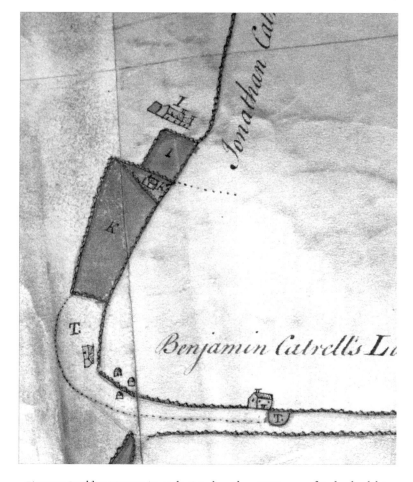

Figure 5 Buckley Mountain as depicted on the c.1757 map of Ewloe lordship (GW 651). A detail showing three pottery kilns. Reproduced with the permission of the Gwysaney Estate and the Flintshire Record Office.

Table 1 Potteries and encroachments noted on Gwysaney maps XI and XII
(after Messham 1956, Appendix C)

Tenant	Encroachment	Description
Benjamin Davies	Map XI: N 1-5	House, pinfold, mug-kiln, crofts
Benjamin Cottrell	Map XI: F 5	Mug-kiln and house
Joseph Codrell's sister	Map XII: 2	Crofts, house, mug-kiln, garden
Thomas Lewis	Map XII: 3, 5, 7, 9	Crofts, gardens, yard, mug-kiln, smithy
Edward Whitley	Map XII: 13	House, garden, mug-kiln
Jonathan Hayes	Map XII: 23	Public house, mug-kiln, garden etc
Peter Ledsham	Map XII: 27, 29	House, mug-kiln, croft

series several kilns are shown but none named, although the reference book notes seven encroachments on Buckley Common which contained 'mug-kilns' (Table 1). The reference book for these maps has become divorced from the maps themselves, and now resides in the National Library of Wales. A synopsis by archivists in the Flintshire Record Office – using the evidence of payments for their surveys made to the well-established Matthews family of Mold – indicates that the maps were drawn between 1779 and 1781 (Thomas 1985).

A further compilation based on map XII, above, was drawn in 1792 to show cottages and encroachments in the lordship and manor of Ewloe and in Ewloe Wood. Though it does show rather randomly some farms lying away from Buckley Mountain, there is a strong probability that any potteries and bottle kilns lying on the enclosed ground will not have been depicted. An undated map in the Gwysaney archives attributed to the early 19th century shows the north-western end of Buckley Mountain, the enclosed land on the south side but north of the stream belonging to General Gascoigne. Four pot kilns are shown but not named, as well as the Bye Pit and Engine Pit. Three small maps of about 1814 (GW/B/555) show encroachments in Ewloe, one map depicting Ewloe Green, the other two linear encroachments along what appear to be drove or roadways. None unfortunately appears to have information directly relevant to the Buckley pottery industry.

The Ordnance Survey surveyors' drawing of the area is late in the sequence of such maps and predates the tithe maps by only five years. It is informative in that six potteries are named, although the map's scale is small, and it is difficult to determine precisely which buildings are indicated. Nevertheless, we can be reasonably certain that three of the six potteries are not found on later maps. The Tithe maps, with Buckley Mountain falling largely in the parish of Hawarden (1841) but with a little on the fringe in Mold (1839), provide limited but useful information. Not surprisingly pottery kilns, with the exception of one at Catherall's Pottery (Site 8), are not shown and buildings are stylistically depicted. Strangely there appears to have been more enclosed ground on Buckley Mountain in the early 1840s than thirty years later.

Even after the tithe surveys, estate mapping continued, usually with very specific purposes in mind. From 1857 is a map of the lands of P Davies Cooke (GW/752) which extends over the countryside to the north of Buckley Mountain. Alltami is shown on its southernmost boundary, and the edge of the mountain with just the one pottery kiln at Willow Grove (Llwyn Helig) near Pinfold Lane. An 1860 tracing (GW/748) is at a large scale (2 chains to the inch, or 1:1584) and shows 'pot works', as well as shafts, limekilns, brick works and a brick kiln. Individual fields and plots are numbered and given acreages, but the accompanying schedule does not appear to have survived; nor is it evident what map provided the original for the tracing. A second 1860 tracing (GW/749) shows land to the north-west of Alltami along the River Wepre and is of interest only in the general context of this study. Much the same can be said of a map from 1863 showing a small part of the Mountain with its focus the Belmont Brickworks and surrounding roads and encroachments.

By the time of the earliest large-scale Ordnance Survey mapping much of Buckley Mountain had been enclosed. The potteries that existed – eight in all – were represented on these maps, either by the depiction of a circular structure, reflecting the presence of a standard kiln, or in two instances as conventional rectangular buildings. In the case of Hayes Pottery (Site 10) near St Matthew's Church, the building was accompanied by two kilns on the map of 1874, though on later editions their outlines had been changed beyond recognition, even if their function remained unaltered. Curiously, this was only named as a pottery on the 1912 map. A second – the Ewloe Pottery (Site 15) – shows no kilns since they were housed within a building, rather than being separate structures.

History and Significance of the Buckley Potteries

Peter Davey

Medieval background

Both archaeological and documentary evidence point to pottery manufacture in the Buckley area during the Middle Ages (Messham 1956; 1989, 169; Prichard 2006, 72). Wasters recovered in field walking in the Ewloe area, just east of the present Buckley boundary, demonstrate the production of pottery and ridge tiles in a coarse highly-fired fabric from around AD 1350 (Harrison and Davey 1977). The market for these wares was within a radius of around 30km from the production sites; this was normal at this period, especially in the regional economic and political focus of Chester. Although urban industries are known, for example in Exeter (Allan 1984; McCarthy and Brooks 1988, 197-8), most medieval potteries were located in rural areas on suitable clay sources within a day's journey from the markets at which they were sold. Whilst at urban centres such as London and Dublin as much as 10% of the pottery consumed was produced at greater distances, often on the continent, it is unusual elsewhere for excavated assemblages to exceed two to five percent of non-local wares (Davey and Hodges 1983, 239-242).

Ewloe wares are found throughout north-east Wales and in west Cheshire. In Chester, the main market, they were able to compete successfully with the long-standing industries based in the central Cheshire ridge. A good example is the assemblage from the Dominican Friary (Axworthy Rutter 1990). During this period Ewloe pottery is of regional significance, but except for the short-lived activity in Rhuddlan (Miles 1977), it is the only medieval production centre known in North Wales.

Early modern developments (c1500-1750)

In Western Europe from the 16th century onwards there was an increase in urbanisation, the development of a larger middle class and marked changes in social structures and manners which led to a rising demand for new types of ceramics both for the table and for food preparation and cooking. These wares required a more advanced kiln design and a more sophisticated range of kiln furniture.

Although many of the coalfields of Britain, including Flintshire, were being exploited for their fuel throughout the Middle Ages, in the two centuries after 1500 the wider potential for industrial development began to be realised (Lloyd Gruffydd 1970; 1971; 1975). As noted above ('Geology') the Coal Measures included clays with a range of specialist properties as well as supplies of minerals such as iron, copper and lead which were often close by. This encouraged their development as centres of industrial innovation, particularly in the iron and ceramic industries.

Coal and fireclays outcropped on Buckley Mountain, and there were superficial boulder clay deposits suitable for pottery making. Fireclays were available which were essential for the provision of saggars in which to protect the finer wares and formed a component in the boulder clays making them generally receptive to higher firing temperatures. Pipe clays allowed the development of local tobacco pipe production, and lead sources for glazing were accessible on Halkyn Mountain, only 8km to the north-west. Most significantly there was direct access to the River Dee, latterly by gravity tramways which had been developed in stages from 1799 for transporting coal and which reached Buckley by 1834. This meant that Buckley pottery could easily be exported by sea and the industry did not depend solely on local over-land markets in Chester and north-east Wales.

The status of the Buckley potters gave them advantages over their contemporaries in some other Coal Measures areas. They were essentially full-time specialist artisans. In other developing ceramic industries, such as that in south Lancashire, for example, pottery making was carried out by farmers as a part-time, seasonal activity that could be fitted in to the farming year (Rowe and Stewart 2014, 11-12). In Buckley the potteries were small-scale, established on encroachments onto the common, and only provided sufficient land for subsistence crops and livestock. Consequently, pottery making was the main source of income.

In contrast to centres such as Wrenthorpe, Yorkshire (Moorhouse and Roberts 1992), Ticknall, Derbyshire (Boyle 2002-3; Spavold and Brown 2005) or Rainford, Lancashire (Rowe and Stewart 2014; Philpott *et al.* 2015) there is no evidence so far for 16th-century pottery making in the Buckley area. The post-medieval ceramic technological package appears to have arrived fully fledged in the middle of the 17th century: high-temperature kilns, the use of fireclays, saggars, slips, lead glazes and moulds. The main products were in thrown red earthenware: lead glazed, yellow slip-trailed bowls, cups and small jugs together with larger, black-glazed storage vessels in both closed and open forms. Less common types included figurines, slipware bowls with *sgraffito* decoration and some buff-bodied slipware. Large press-moulded chargers were produced from early on, with some mould fragments surviving. Mottled wares became important in the latter part of the century - the Buckley potters producing a wide range of forms in addition to the ubiquitous tankards. Tobacco pipes, using local clay in Broseley-style moulds were produced from around 1680 to 1720 (Cropper 1906; Bentley, Davey and Harrison 1979; 1980; Davey 1981; Davidson and Davey 1982; Higgins 1983, 1985).

Although north-east Wales and west Cheshire remained the most consistent markets for the Buckley potters, evidence from archaeological excavations further afield, especially in the Isle of Man and Ireland, demonstrate that significant quantities of identifiable coarse ware and slipware, both thrown and press-moulded, were being shipped overseas. It is likely that a good proportion of the black-glazed pottery and slipware present in these assemblages will have derived from Buckley; but these technological types still need definitive characterisation to discriminate between the different production centres (*cf.* White 2012; Davey *et al.* 2014).

The later potteries (c1750-1945)

Developments within the wider ceramic industry in Britain had a significant effect on the Buckley potteries. The establishment of the canal system provided land-locked centres such as those in Staffordshire with greatly extended markets. During the 18th century technical innovations that included the development of white salt-glazed stoneware, porcelain, cream-ware and pearl ware placed the potteries of the English Midlands in a pre-eminent position not solely within Britain but also in terms of world-wide ceramic trade.

The effect of these developments on existing Coal Measures industries was profound. The market for the finer white-bodied earthenware and stoneware had effectively been captured by Stoke-on-Trent, so that such centres had to diversify or fail. In the case of Buckley, a range of responses can be seen. One segment of the potteries continued to operate on a small scale, as extended family businesses, well into the 20th century (Prichard 2006, 79-82). These tended to focus mainly on the production of black-glazed kitchen and dairy wares which because of their bulk, low value and relatively high transport costs, could compete with Staffordshire in the local markets. Some of these small-scale potteries were able to develop niche markets in souvenirs and domestic accessories, such as furniture casters (eg Davey 1975a, nos. 31-44).

From around 1750 potters began to exploit the local fireclays in a more extensive manner. Catheralls and Hancocks, in particular, created more integrated industrial complexes, with part-ownership of collieries and lead mines and well as brick, tile and pottery production (Prichard 2006, 77-78; Lyons 1986; Davey 1975a, nos. 48-54).

Three main types of market existed during this period, with different potteries specialising in different products: local, tourist and industrial.

The potteries continued to supply the Chester market and north Wales with black-glazed kitchen ware of all kinds and a range of low-cost tableware, such as crudely made press-moulded plates (eg Tyler 1983, 21). They also evolved a series of rusticated and *sgraffito* decorated ware with local, often personalised legends, including tobacco jars, plant pots, castors, candle sticks, shaving mugs and puzzle jugs (eg Davey 1975a, nos. 22-37). Some of the coarse wares were probably traded further afield, but they are difficult to distinguish from equivalent wares from centres such as Glasgow, Liverpool, Ironbridge and Stoke-on-Trent. Finds of the other wares are very rare outside Chester and north-east Wales. In the 20th century some Buckley potters responded to national and international changes in taste and attempted to produce art pottery, including items with *art nouveau* designs (Davey 1975a, no. 46). Some smaller potteries specialised in tourist wares, often using legends or quotations in the Welsh language (Davey 1975a, nos. 61-63). These were in demand in Chester and the seaside resorts of the Dee estuary and north Wales. The wares involved include tea-pots, cups and saucers, milk jugs, salts and sugar bowls. Specific domestic items such as door handles and buttons (the latter for Browns of Chester) were also produced.

Pottery needed to be carefully packed for transport. In some cases, bracken was used as a packing material, while some potteries apparently kept a stand of rye straw for the same purpose (Hartley 1974, 175).

The main firms, such as Catheralls and Hancocks, made refractory bricks for a variety of purposes, such as roof furniture, blast furnace linings and ships boiler linings, malt kiln floors, crucibles, acid resistant pipes and junctions for the lead industry, as well as low value pottery, including the latest devolved forms of slipware and crude stoneware (Bentley 1979; Lyons 1986, 40; Crew 2002; 2003). They operated on an industrial scale.

History of archaeological research

Excavation

The first formal excavation was carried out in 1954 on part of Prescot's Pottery (Barton 1956). This produced a range of 18th-century production waste dominated by black-glazed wares, but no structures. Between 1973 and 1985 Bentley and Harrison explored sites at Brookhill and Pinfold Lane (Sites 1 and 2 respectively) in some detail. At Brookhill a wide range of 17th- and 18th-century wares were recovered together with 13 small, shallow kiln bases (Bentley 1982). At Pinfold lane they collected a wider range of 18th-century slip-wares and kiln furniture, but no clear structures were uncovered (Davey 1987).

In 1974 the Flintshire Historical Society sampled the waste tip of Hancock's Pottery (Site 14; Bentley 1973; Davey 1976). Finds included a range of industrial wares as well as later forms of black-glazed wares, thrown and pressed slip-wares.

More recent excavations in Buckley have been initiated through the planning process in response to development pressures. In 1984 a larger area was opened in Pinfold Lane; this revealed the brick foundations of two kilns, an ore-crushing pit and two clay soaking pits (McNeil 1984; 1985a; 1985b; Knight 2001). In 1986 geophysical survey and trial excavations were carried out on a site where it was believed that medieval pottery and wasters had been recovered. No structures were located but further medieval wasters were found (Weetman 1986; Maude 1986) and it was therefore believed that the site of a medieval pottery (Site 18) had been identified. A more recent geophysical survey also failed to locate any possible kiln structures (Hankinson 2015) and it was subsequently realized that the original finds scatter was recovered from the field to the north and that it was there that the medieval pottery was probably located; some irregularities are evident on the LiDAR coverage for this field but they are more likely to relate to later industrial activity than the pottery.

In 1990 an exploratory excavation examined two geophysical anomalies to the north of the Catherall Pottery (Site 8) but failed to recover any production elements, whether structures or artefacts (Jones 1990). In 2000, excavations on the site of Lewis's pottery (Site 5) revealed two six-flued brick kilns (Figure

Figure 6 The blunger excavated at Taylor's Pottery in 2005 (Photo courtesy of Earthworks Archaeology).

15), domestic accommodation, workshop and drying floor - by far the most extensive set of pottery-related structures so far located in Buckley (Earthworks 2000; Dodd 2003). In 2005 a brick-founded blunger was located during exploratory excavations near to the site of Taylor's Pottery (Site 3) - the first of its type to be identified in Buckley (Figure 6; Earthworks 2005). In 2017 a strip and sampling exercise carried out close to Lamb's Pottery (Site 9) located pits and features containing significant quantities of material waste from pottery production including late 18th or early 19th-century slipwares and kiln furniture (Dodd 2017).

Finally, in 2014 and 2015 a community-based project was carried out by CPAT on the part of Price's Pottery (Site 11) that lay within the curtilage of Elfed School and provides a substantial component of this monograph (Hankinson 2014; Hankinson and Culshaw 2014, Watson and Culshaw 2015). Small-scale investigations were subsequently undertaken by CPAT at Brookhill (Site 1) (Hankinson 2017).

Survey

In 1974 the Flintshire Archaeological Society established the Buckley Clay Industries Research Committee which carried out a field survey initially identifying 16 pottery production sites (Davey 1974) and a further three sites in the following year (Davey 1975b; 1976a; 1976b; 1976c). Modern map regression analysis carried out by CPAT has increased this number to 31 (Jones 2014) which are listed in Appendix 2.

Publication

To date, no coherent, comprehensive account exists of the potteries or their products. Whilst the Messham (1956) paper and the potteries chapter in Prichard's *The Making of Buckley and District* (2006) provide good overviews of the historical evidence, the pottery itself has been far less well served. The Clay Industries Research Committee produced a booklet, *Buckley Pottery*, that included 81 photographs, including some of the excavated pieces (Davey 1975a). Unfortunately, although the complete vessels were collected in Flintshire a few of them have subsequently been shown to have been made elsewhere. In 1983 a comprehensive exhibition was assembled at the Mostyn Art Gallery in Llandudno, deriving objects from a wide number of public and private collections, and then circulated widely in the region. The handbook written to accompany this display (Tyler 1983) provides an excellent account of the industry, its use of raw materials and production techniques. It also included 26 illustrations, many of which were in colour, but no catalogue of the exhibition itself.

The excavated material is even less well published. There has been no formal account of the archaeological evidence from the main sites and only relatively small samples of their products. The Barton excavations involved a very narrow range of forms and his identification of Buckley-type black-glazed wares found in Chester and as far as the New World as 'Buckley Ware' has dogged all subsequent research. A small group from Pinfold Lane (Site 2), published in *Post-Medieval Archaeology* in 1975, alerted ceramicists to the wider technological range of Buckley products but only involved nine vessels (Davey 1975b).

There are a few synthetic studies on the material from the excavations. In particular, accounts of bestiary wares (Lloyd-Gruffydd 1980; Longworth 2004) and the social status of the potters and their decorative designs (Longworth 2005).

Given the very large quantities of pottery excavated from Buckley sites since 1954 only relatively small groups have been published. The two most extensive presentations are those by Amery and Davey (1979) involving 143 ceramic items from Brookhill (Site 1) with many complete profiles and Davey (1987) with 76 objects from Pinfold Lane (Site 2) including kiln furniture, separators, moulds and clay pipes. But in both papers the selection of the pottery to be illustrated and discussed is random and not related to the sites' archaeology or stratigraphy. Even in the publication of a modern professional excavation such as that at Lewis's Pottery (Site 4) in 2000 (Dodd 2003), only a single ceramic object is figured.

Much useful material remains unpublished. The sequence of 20 unpublished reports by Bentley and Harrison covering the period 1972 to 1985 provide invaluable detail of Sites 1, 2 and 14 and their products. The same is true of the unpublished reports produced by CPAT and Earthworks Archaeology in connection with planning-related assessment on or close to Site 3 (Earthworks 2005), Site 5 (Dodd 2000), Site 9 (Dodd 2017), Site 11 (Hankinson and Jones 2014) and Site 18 (Maude 1986; Weetman 1986; Hankinson 2015).

Some very useful and detailed studies have been produced as University diplomas and dissertations such as Rutter (1977) on Site 11, Morgan (1978) on Site 19, Philpott (1978) on Site 14 and Amery (1979) and

Longworth (1999) on the *sgraffito* from Site 1. All these studies can be accessed in the collection of the Flintshire Record Office in Hawarden or in the National Museums Liverpool (Cook and Longworth 2000).

There are also a few synthetic studies, which have sought to define and identify Buckley pottery. These have taken two forms. First has been physical analysis of the fabric and decoration to determine technique and provenance by comparison with contemporary production centres elsewhere in the UK (Davey and Longworth 2001; Longworth and Davey 2016). Second, scientific techniques have been brought to bear: using thin-section analysis of the clays and fabric (Davidson 1982), and through x-ray fluorescence (XRF) chemical analysis (Davey *et al.* 2014). The most important attempt to synthesise the evidence for the sites themselves is by Jones (2014) in *The Buckley potteries: an assessment of survival and potential*, detailing the results of a Cadw-funded study, the core of which forms a key element in the present volume.

Significance

The Buckley potteries represent the most significant concentration of evidence for the post-medieval ceramic industry in Wales, with multiple sites and continuity of production from the mid-17th to the mid-20th century. The recent reassessment of the Buckley potteries (Jones 2014) concluded that while the location of the majority of potteries has now been established, most have sadly been lost, or at least significantly disturbed by later development, while only a few are thought to retain significant archaeological potential. From a ceramic research perspective, they offer possibilities for the study of a set of inter-related issues such as:

- The inception and process of industrialisation within the industry
- The development of kiln technology
- Competition, adaption and innovation
- Assimilation and adoption of cultural norms
- Regionalisation and trade
- The characterisation of Coal Measures clays and lead sources by scientific methods

The Buckley potteries are much more than regionally significant. In the 17th and early 18th centuries they are important for the study of archaeological assemblages not only in Chester, west Cheshire and north-east Wales but also for the whole Irish Sea area including north-west Wales, north and east Ireland and the Isle of Man. From 1750 until the mid-20th century specialist Buckley refractory wares are found in the Americas, Africa and beyond.

Recent Excavations
Brookhill Pottery (Site 1), 2016

Richard Hankinson

Brookhill is the earliest post-medieval pottery known in Buckley and was excavated extensively by Bentley between 1974 and 1985 (see Figure 7), revealing up to 15 kiln bases, ten of which were defined by shallow depressions filled with ash, coal dust, kiln furniture and wasters. These appear to have been clamp kilns with infilled material providing a firm refractory floor which, being porous, also acted as an underfloor flue. Two smaller kilns were set directly on the ground (Amery and Davey 1979, 51). The kilns all had internal diameters of between 1.5m and 2m (Gruffydd 2010, 88). The site has been dated by the material found during Bentley's excavations to around 1640-1720. The pottery lies to the north-east of Pinfold Lane, between an industrial estate and the line of a former railway (SJ 2757 6462); it occupies an overgrown plot within which the ruins of a 19th-century house and stable can be identified.

The earliest wares from Brookhill include complex slip-decorated thrown bowls, executed in both *sgraffito* and trailing techniques, porringers with press-moulded handles, a female figurine and large tripod cooking vessels. Later wares include mottled ware tankards and bowls, slipware dishes and black- and brown-glazed cups and storage vessels (Davey 1976a, 18).

The Bentley archive is now curated by National Museums Liverpool and an interrogation of the original site drawings has shed further light on the extent of Bentley's investigations and the layout of the remains which were revealed, enabling a more accurate plan to be produced than has so far been possible. It should be noted, however, that there appear to have been inherent problems with the site grid, such that successive seasons of excavation may not have been located correctly with respect to each other. The overall plan presented in Figure 7 has been derived from Bentley's drawings as a 'best fit' and shows the general distribution of the kilns and other structures, although it should not be taken as being metrically accurate.

In order to assess the surviving potential of the site, as well as confirm the location of some features identified by Bentley, small-scale investigations were undertaken by CPAT in 2016. The original intention had been to carry out a programme of geophysics in the area surrounding that excavated by Bentley, which could be used to inform trial investigations, with the aim of identifying the extent of the pottery, although this was not possible as permission was not forthcoming from the owner. Instead, work focussed on two hand-excavated trenches (Trenches 1 and 2) within a garden plot to the south-west of the main area of the pottery and two 1m-square test pits (Trenches 3 and 4) in an area of scrub further to the south-west (Figure 7). The test pits produced artefacts contemporary with Brookhill Pottery, but no significant archaeological features and consequently are not discussed further below.

It was not intended to completely excavate any layers or features that were revealed, rather that it was sufficient to identify surviving elements of the pottery to determine the nature and extent of Bentley's excavations and assess the preservation of the archaeology.

Trench 1

The trench was aligned roughly east/west and measured 8.1m by 1.4m. The earliest features identified are likely to be two short sections of stone wall. Insufficient lengths of either were revealed to allow their stratigraphic relationships to be determined, but they appeared to be on the approximate alignment of the walls of the 'old white cottage' that occupied the site prior to 1900. The walls were probably butted by the earliest discrete layer which was recorded, an orange-brown clay-silt that contained some post-medieval pottery sherds; this was not investigated further to ensure that its relationships to adjoining layers were retained.

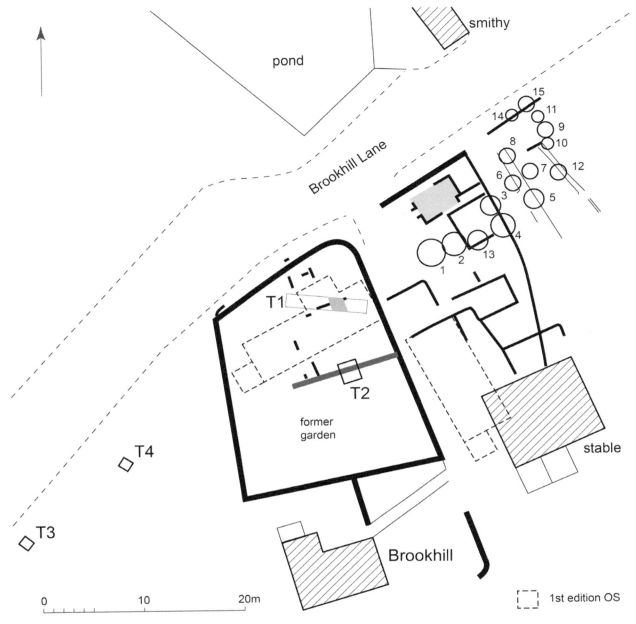

Figure 7 Plan of Brookhill Pottery based on Bentley's original records, showing the location of the 2016 trenches.

Throughout the trench this layer was sealed beneath a 50mm-thick deposit of white lime mortar/plaster containing small stones and fragments of brick and slate. Occasional lumps of white clay were also observed in the layer, which might be related to clay pipe manufacture. The layer is perhaps best interpreted as either demolition rubble from the cottage, or perhaps floors within it that may equate with those identified in this location by Bentley.

Later activity consisted of a brick and stone path, 1.1m wide, which had been laid within a shallow, flat-bottomed trench. A similar path was still visible at the time of excavation further to the south. This was associated with the ruinous house built in 1900, and it is probable that the two paths were connected or at least part of the same phase of landscaping. The survival of both paths imply that significant sections of this area were not excavated by Bentley and may therefore retain undisturbed archaeological deposits.

Trench 2

The trench, which measured 1.8m by 1.8m, was located approximately 5m to the south of Trench 1, and oriented north-south/east-west. Part of a possible wall foundation was revealed, aligned north-north-west/south-south-east and varying between 0.5m and 0.75m wide, with a fill composed almost exclusively of pieces of greyish sandstone. On the south side this had been cut through a layer of buff-brown sandy clay, while the north side was cut through a layer of orange-brown silt. Both were sealed beneath a deposit of dark grey slag, up to 0.1m thick, which seemed to have been laid as a deliberate surface.

The wall foundation had been cut by a culvert, aligned east/west, which had a flat base and measured 1.14m wide by 0.46m deep (Figure 8). This was lined by blocks of buff-coloured sandstone, leaving a central void which had been capped by larger stone slabs. The base of the culvert contained a thin layer of silt. The stone lining appeared to have been covered by a cap of reddish clay, up to 0.2m thick, which presumably acted to seal the culvert, although only part remained.

The culvert had previously been identified by Bentley, who had replaced the stone capping and covered it with a plastic sheet to protect the archaeology when the excavations were backfilled. Although he described it as a drain the dark red colour of the clay at its base suggested that it had been affected by heat, although from what source the colour originated is unclear.

The pottery

The assemblage was very fragmentary and the sherd sizes generally small, while all the material recovered was residual in contexts which were not stratified securely, the majority deriving from topsoil or backfill

Figure 8 Brookhill 2016, Trench 2 from the east, showing the culvert after excavation with remnants of the probable wall foundation to either side. CPAT 4260-0035.

Table 2 Summary quantification of the pottery from Brookhill 2016, trenches 1 and 2

Type of ware	No sherds		Total
	Trench 1	Trench 2	
Blackware	790	290	1080
Unglazed sherds	55	16	71
Slip-trailed ware	195	85	280
Lead-glazed ware	172	54	232
Developed White ware	62	68	130
Coarseware	77	10	87
Mottled ware	34	22	56
Saggar	43	9	52
Brown ware	31	19	50
Agate ware	6	26	32
Stoneware	6	6	12
Pearlware	1	4	5
Mocha ware	0	5	5
Creamware	1	2	3
Sgraffito	0	2	2
Industrial Slipware	1	0	1
Tin glazed earthenware	0	1	1
Ironstone ware	0	1	1
TOTAL	1474	620	2100

of the previous excavations. While there were a significant number of obvious wasters it was difficult to determine how much of the pottery finds were the product of the nearby kilns. There was a small collection of 19th-century pottery, largely teawares, which were contemporary with the later cottage, while at least some of the general assemblage of earthenwares is also likely to be contemporary with later occupation.

Trench 1 produced the largest amount of pottery, totalling 1,474 sherds. A range of different ceramic types and forms have been identified, including a small fragment of a sgraffito dish from context 4 and part of a possible dish with joggled decoration from context 1, with a tentative date of 1720-1760, although this is clearly residual and was not necessarily produced at Brookhill. A significant quantity of mostly unglazed coarsewares were also present, using a yellow fire clay fabric which was very similar to the saggars, but included very distinctive rim forms (see Figure 9). The only kiln furniture consisted of two spacers or props.

Trench 2 also produced a significant collection of ceramics, totalling 620 sherds. These included part of the rim of a dish with sgraffito decoration, and four sherds of fineware with joggled, one of which was part of a hollow-ware rim and probably dated to 1690-1720. Twenty-four sherds of agate-bodied ware were also recovered, including two handles of possible posset cups which could date to broadly the same period. Another interesting find was part of a circular ceramic object (see Figure 10) made from fire clay, on which the name 'George' was inscribed, with what seemed to be the start of a surname following it; the surviving segment represented about 25% of the complete object which would have been approximately 330mm in diameter. It might be speculated that this was the lid of a saggar inscribed with the name of the potter whose items it would have covered.

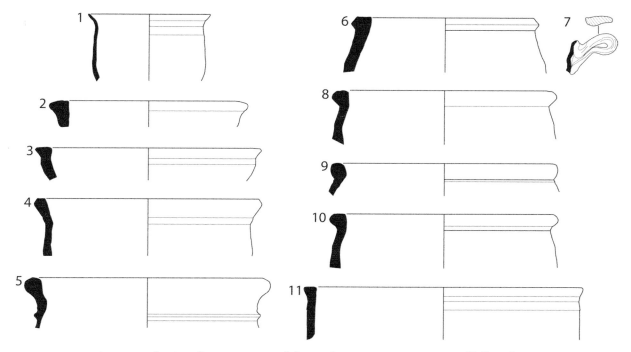

Figure 9 A selection of pottery recovered during the 2016 excavations at Brookhill. Scale 1:4.

Catalogue of pottery from the 2016 excavations at Brookhill Pottery.

1. Fine, blackware rim sherd, slightly out-turned. Glaze stops on external surface where the vessel body starts to curve inwards towards the base. 130mm diameter. Red earthenware fabric.
2. Red, fireclay cooking pot rim. 210mm diameter.
3. Buff fireclay cooking pot rim. 240mm diameter.
4. Buff fireclay cooking pot rim with red slip wash. 240mm diameter.
5. Brown ware storage vessel rim. Glaze to interior, red slip wash to external. 260mm diameter. Red earthenware fabric. Possibly 1640-1720.
6. Buff fireclay cooking pot rim, with red slip wash. Some blobs of brown glaze to exterior. 195mm diameter.
7. Red earthenware looped, side handle. Handle is unglazed but the body of the vessel, which is wheel thrown shows traces of brown glaze on the interior and possible buff slip decoration.
8. Buff fireclay cooking pot rim. 240mm diameter.
9. Buff fireclay cooking pot with rounded rim. 240mm diameter.
10. Buff fireclay cooking pot rim with red slip wash. 240mm diameter.
11. Buff fireclay cooking pot rim. 300mm diameter.

Conclusions

The limited investigations provided some useful information relating to the location of features previously revealed by Bentley. It also produced an

Figure 10 Part of an inscribed circular object made from fire clay, possibly a saggar lid, from context 55. Scale 1:4.

assemblage of pottery which fits broadly within the date ranges of c. 1640-1720 previously attributed to the site.

From Bentley's records, it appears that much of the area where the kilns were identified was excavated fully down to the sandstone bedrock. However, the same cannot be said for the other areas which he investigated. Evidence from Trenches 1 and 2 revealed that both retained *in situ* evidence for significant features and deposits, although it was uncertain whether these related directly to the pottery. It is also worth noting that he identified features, including two kilns (Figure 7, 14 and 15), emerging from the bank along the south-east side of Brookhill Lane, suggesting that the thoroughfare, at least in its present form, is a later feature which truncated the north-western side of the pottery.

Taylor's Pottery (Site 3), 2005

Leigh Dodd

In 2005 an evaluation was undertaken by Earthworks Archaeology in connection with a planning application to develop a vacant plot to the south-east of Taylor's Pottery, the earthwork remains of which are one of only two scheduled potteries in the Buckley area.

Figure 11 The layout of Taylor's Pottery, showing the location of the evaluation trenches

Background

The site occupies an encroachment onto the common and is recorded on the Ewloe Lordship map of 1757, which shows a single kiln on the common and a rectangular building within an enclosure. The *c.* 1780 Ewloe Estate map (no XII) lists the tenant as Joseph Codrell's sister, describing the land as occupied by crofts, house, mug-kiln and garden. Later records indicate that the pottery was operated by the Taylor family (John Taylor in 1815; Taylor and Son in 1860; and Charles Taylor in 1886).

The pottery complex straddled both sides of Alltami Road and the 1874 mapping shows two kilns, a 'mill' and a number of potters' workshops and houses. To the north-east of the road, located on the common, the map depicts two ponds, likely to be clay pans, linked by a watercourse, as well as a kiln which had been recorded in 1860 as a brick kiln. Later editions of the Ordnance Survey mapping, in 1899 and 1912, show that the pottery was still active with minor changes to the layout.

The site of two kilns, chimneys, drying sheds and blunging pits lie in rough pasture, an area which is now a scheduled monument (FL 165). A range of other structures and features to the south-east are partly beneath later buildings, although some, including workers' housing, may be incorporated into the extant buildings. The slight earthworks of clay pans, or settling tanks, can still be discerned among the vegetation on the north-east side of the road.

Excavations

The evaluation comprised two trenches, each 2m wide, measuring 13m and 17m in length. Trench 1 was positioned along the frontage with Alltami Road, and revealed a sequence of redeposited, mixed clay layers assumed to be infilling a large, square pond shown by the Ordnance Survey in 1871. The nature of these deposits suggested that the pond may have been a clay pan, a shallow pool in which clay was stored and weathered down prior to being refined for pottery production at the nearby kiln complex (Bentley 1982, 18). Several clay pans still survive as slight earthworks on the opposite side of the road.

Trench 2 uncovered the partial remains of a circular, brick-built structure, also depicted in 1871, which was recorded then as a 'mill'. The structure measured around 5m in diameter and was defined by an outer wall of brick (33) three courses deep (0.6m wide) (Figures 6 and 12). Some of the bricks were fused

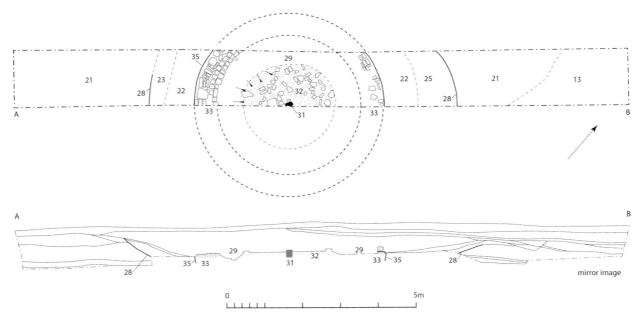

Figure 12 The excavated remains of the brick-built blunger at Taylor's Pottery.

together by glaze and they had clearly been reused from a kiln structure; large lumps of fuel slag were also used in the construction. The wall had been built in a foundation cut (35), filled by a deposit of pinkish brown clay (36).

The centre of the structure was occupied by a brick and stone floor (32) around 2.5m in diameter, which had been laid on a bed of pink clay (34) containing fragments of probable lime mortar. The remains of a wooden post (31), c. 0.2m in diameter, was set into the middle of the floor, presumably forming a central pivot. A shallow trough (29), 0.6m to 0.8m wide and 0.14m deep, occupied the area between the outer brick wall (33) and the central floor (32). The trough was filled by a mixed yellow and grey clay (24).

A large pit (28), around 10m across and 0.5m deep, predated the brick structure and had been backfilled with a series of deposits containing brick and pottery, including a c. 0.1m-thick deposit of crushed orange ceramic material (probably pottery) in a matrix of pink clay (22).

When the structure fell out of use, between 1869 and 1870 and the late 1880s according to the cartographic evidence, pottery waste, including some large sherds from black-glazed coarse earthenware storage jars and similar vessels, continued to accumulate within this hollow and sealed the remains of the structure.

The Finds

The post-medieval pottery recovered during the fieldwork represents products which can be considered typical of the Buckley potteries during the 19th and 20th centuries. The vessel types represented are generally utilitarian in function and comprise large pancheons of a type used in the preparation of dough, dairy-based food products and similar food types. These vessels are glazed internally with a (sometimes) lustrous black glaze which draws its colouring from the iron-rich slip often applied beneath. Black-glazed storage jars are also represented in both tall cylindrical form and a more rounded type, which is often used in brewing, or with a pierced bung-hole near the base, as a cistern; although none of the vessels here exhibited a bung-hole. Handles, where present, are of the horizontally applied lug-handle type, located just below the vessel rim. Bowls coated internally with a clear, brown glaze were also present in the overall assemblage; some vessels were decorated internally with trailed cream slip designs.

Close dating of these types of wares is difficult as such utilitarian vessel forms can be quite long-lived. However, the assemblage as a whole is likely to date from perhaps the mid-19th to the early 20th centuries. A single mottled ware-type sherd, recovered from the stratigraphically earliest deposit, may date to the first half of the 18th century, perhaps suggesting potting, or at least occupation, within this general area at that time. Much, if not all, of the pottery recovered during the evaluation was clearly dumped waste material from nearby kilns and, as indicated by ware marks on at least one vessel, probable domestic occupation. Indeed, many of the contexts encountered were clearly imported and consisted of waste clay, cinders and other materials resulting from nearby pottery manufacturing.

A small collection of kiln furniture was also present, comprising conical-shaped stilts used to support glazed vessels during firing and often used to support smaller vessels within larger ones, and separators or spacers formed by squeezing a lump of soft clay in the palm of the hand.

1. Bowl, 380mm diameter, with clear, brown-glazed interior. Trench 1, context 5.
2. Large storage jar, 380mm diameter, black-glazed internally and part way down exterior. Hand-print in glaze on exterior surface. Trench 2, context 12.
3. Bowl with internal and external clear brown-glazed surfaces. Trench 2, context 13.
4. Bowl with internal and external clear brown-glazed surfaces. Trench 2, context 13.
5. Pancheon, black-glazed internally. Trench 2, context 23.
6. Lid-seated storage jar, 190mm diameter, with lug-handle. Black glazed internally and externally. Trench 2, context 12.
7. Bowl, 300mm diameter, with internal clear-brown glaze. Trench 2, context 12.

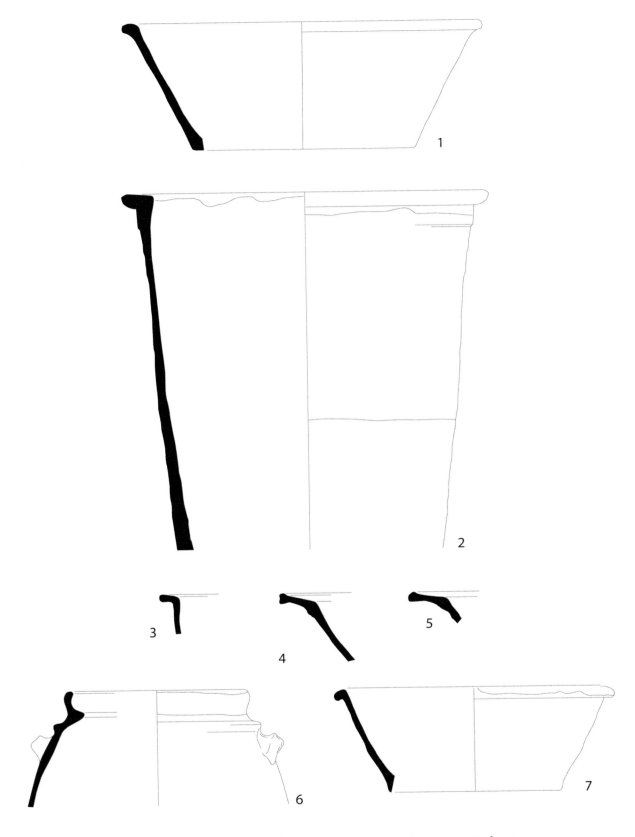

Figure 13 Pottery recovered from the 2005 excavations at Taylor's pottery. Scale 1:4.

Conclusions

The results from the small-scale excavations confirmed the late 19th-century map evidence, showing that a range of features associated with Taylor's Pottery survive beyond the confines of the scheduled area. Of particular significance were the remains of a circular brick-built structure, identified as a 'mill' by the Ordnance Survey, which is believed to have been a blunger. The apparatus was used for refining clay and was probably powered by a mule or small pony. Clay was mixed with water in a trough within which paddles or tines rotated around a central timber pivot to break down lumps of clay into a slurry to remove stones and sand, which sank to the bottom. The slurry would then have been drained into clay pans to settle and dray. To date this is the only such structure to have been excavated in the Buckley area.

Lewis's Pottery (Site 5), 2000

Leigh Dodd

Introduction

In March 2000 an archaeological evaluation was carried out by Earthworks Archaeology in advance of a proposed residential development on the site of Lewis's Pottery (Fig. 1, Site 5; SJ 2746 6516) (Earthworks 2000). At the time of the evaluation the site was unoccupied waste ground but had been used as a timber yard until recently. A second phase of excavation later that year investigated a more extensive area, uncovering significant, well-preserved remains of a kiln and pottery building dating from the mid-18th century to the mid-19th century, as well as evidence for earlier potting activity (Dodd 2003).

Background

A pottery was clearly in operation here by 1757, when the Lordship of Ewloe map depicts a kiln and a range of buildings, identifying this as 'Robert Codrell's tenement'. By 1781, however, the pottery was operated by Thomas Lewis, who continued until 1799 when it seems to have been taken over by his son, John Lewis (senior), who worked the pottery until 1835 after which he was succeeded by his son, also

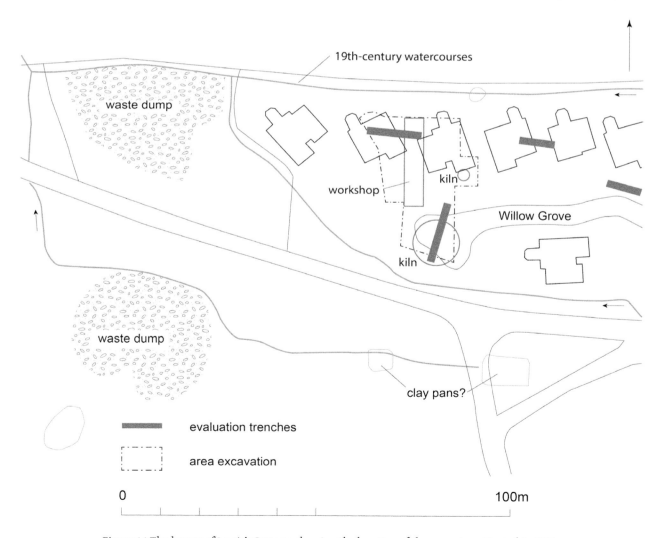

Figure 14 The layout of Lewis's Pottery, showing the location of the areas investigated in 2000.

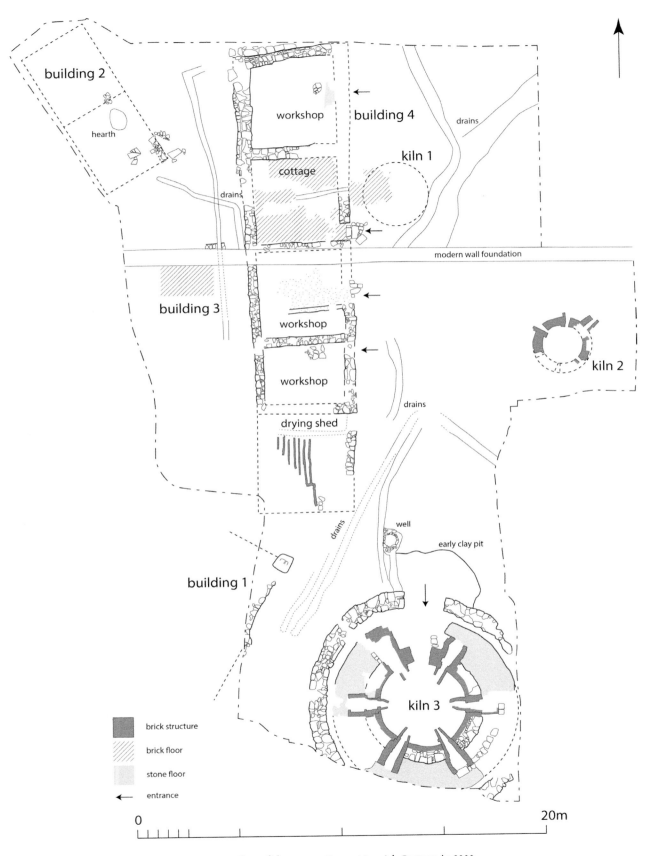

brick structure
brick floor
stone floor
← entrance

0   20m

Figure 15 Plan of the excavations at Lewis's Pottery in 2000.

named John, and later by his daughter Mary. During Mary's tenancy the pottery was worked by George Powell, son of another potter, Samuel Powell of Bolton, who had a pottery nearby (Site 15) (Messham 1956, 42). By the early 20th century the site was occupied by John Hughes. It should be noted that despite there being potteries run by John Lewis Senior and Junior (Site 4) the evidence suggests that they may not have been father and son as, according to Messham (1956, 42) John Lewis Junior died in 1831.

Cartographic sources clearly show the presence of a circular kiln and an adjacent building, probably a cottage or workshop. The layout of the pottery appears unchanged by 1884, the mapping at that time also depicting a small square structure east of the pottery building and what is likely to be a waste dump some 60m to the west. A small pond is shown to the north of the pottery, positioned along a watercourse, associated with a well next to Willow Cottage, while a second stream or channel is shown to the south. Two rectangular features are located on the common, south of the pottery, which are likely to be clay pans, linked by another small watercourse. A small quantity of 19th-century pottery and kiln furniture was found on the edge of the common opposite the site in January 1975 (Davey 1976a, 21).

Excavation

During the summer of 2000 an area measuring approximately 20m by 40m was excavated, the results of which suggest three broad phases of potting activity.

Late 17th century to early 18th century

The earliest activity on the site comprised plough scars cutting into the natural clay subsoil, together with a soil layer containing clay tobacco pipe bowls dated to the late 17th century, and an undated field boundary ditch. The earliest evidence for potting activities consisted of the scant remains of what is likely to be a small kiln (Kiln 1), represented by an area of reddened clay, measuring up to c. 1.3m by 1.8m, together with a small number of fused bricks. Although practically all the structural vestiges of this feature had been removed by later activity, the slightly curving alignment of the surviving bricks suggest that they were part of the outer wall, or possibly the external edge of a floor, for a kiln.

The partial remains of two buildings (Buildings 1 and 2) also probably date from this period. In the south-west corner of the excavated area the foundations of a wall were traced for around 5.0m, aligned north-east to south-west. At the north-eastern end was a large posthole containing a post-pad in the base, formed by two flat stones. The timber had evidently been removed, rather than rotting *in situ*, and the backfill consisted of red clay containing fragments of crushed pottery. Although no internal features or floor surfaces could be identified it seemed likely that the interior lay to the west of the foundation. The relatively insubstantial nature of the foundation, together with the presence of the posthole, suggest that the superstructure for the building is likely to have been timber-framed, set on a low sleeper wall. There was no evidence to suggest the function of the building or confirm its association with the kiln.

The remains of the second building were equally fragmentary, although partial wall footings and a series of postholes suggest a structure some 8.0m or so in length and c. 3.50m wide, comprising two rooms, the southern of which contained a small hearth. This was subjected to archaeomagnetic dating techniques that returned a last firing date of c. 1660 to 1690 (GeoQuest 2000b), while the excavation recovered a clay tobacco pipe from the hearth, dated to the period c. 1690-1720, comparing favourably with the later end of the archaeomagnetic date range.

A number of pits and drainage gullies were also identified which are likely to date to this period of activity, containing black-glazed and trailed slipware vessels (although seemingly not wasters), together with stamped clay tobacco pipe bowls of c. 1680-1720. A pit partially sealed beneath the hovel wall of a large, later kiln (Kiln 3), produced wasters that included a black-glazed bowl and a spouted pipkin suggestive of earlier manufacture on the site, possibly during the late 17th or early 18th centuries.

Early to mid-18th century

Firm evidence for the establishment of a potting complex within the excavation area during the first half of the 18th century is provided by the remains of a small, brick-built kiln (Kiln 2). The surviving structural elements comprised a circular brick oven wall, c. 0.50m wide, with an external diameter of c. 2.90m, enclosing the remains of a brick stacking floor, c. 1.80m in diameter. The southern part of the kiln had been largely removed by later activity. The bricks used in its construction measured c. 230mm by 110mm by 50mm, with only one to two courses remaining. The bonding agent used was a gritty clay that had been heated through the firing of the kiln to a brick-red colour and had become very friable. Six fireboxes were set at regularly-spaced intervals, each extending out from the kiln wall for up to c. 0.60m, their positions being represented largely by brick scaring and coal fuel slag patches. However, one firebox was almost complete, being of rectilinear form, measuring c. 0.80m in length and c. 0.70- 0.90m wide externally, enclosing an internal fuel/fire area measuring c. 0.20m wide. The walls of the firebox then tapered inwards to form the flue throat, passing through the oven wall and tapering further to a narrow flue aperture c. 0.12m wide, which opened into the firing chamber of the oven. The kiln had been constructed on a levelling deposit of coal fragments and cinders that produced a clay tobacco pipe of a type datable to the period c. 1710-1720. This, together with the kilns' absence from the earliest cartographic sources, suggests that it was in operation during the period c. 1710-1750.

The remains of a brick floor, located in the western half of the excavation, suggest the presence of a building (Building 3) which may be contemporary with the kiln and is thought to date from the first half of the 18th century. The floor survived within an area measuring c. 1.50m north-south by c. 2.60m east-west and had been constructed using mostly half-bricks, measuring 140mm by 140mm by 80mm. It was almost certainly associated with the scant remains of at least two stone wall foundations, forming the north and south sides of the building. Coal fragments and dust encountered on the surface of the brick floor suggest that this structure may have functioned as a fuel store, perhaps used in the firing of Kiln 2.

A large sub-circular pit, lying partly beneath the later Kiln 3, may have functioned as a clay quarry pit. The fills contained sherds from warped and wasted pottery vessels, along with a small quantity of clay tobacco pipe stems, one of which had part of a tailed-heel dating it stylistically to the late 17th or early 18th century.

Mid-18th century to mid-19th century

By the later 1750s a well organised pottery complex had been established incorporating a workshop/ cottage and a single, large pottery kiln (Kiln 3) of updraught type. Cartographic sources suggest that this development of the site had taken place by c. 1757 and the layout of the site essentially remained unchanged for perhaps a century.

The excavations uncovered a near complete plan of the kiln base, demonstrating that it was probably of beehive type and consisted of a circular, brick-built firing chamber, 4.1m in diameter, with an internal floor of baked clay and a single walk-in entrance. Six fireboxes were spaced evenly around its circumference, each around 2.50m long overall and measuring 1.m wide at the outer end, while tapering to 0.25-0.30m within the firing chamber. Alternating brick and clay floors lay between the fireboxes, the brick flooring presumably used to provide a working surface upon which to stack fuel for firing (Figure 16). The firing chamber was surrounded by the foundations for a circular hovel, measured 11.75m in diameter.

To the north-west of the kiln the excavations revealed the foundations for a rectangular building (Building 4), 21.95m long and up to 5.58m wide, which was divided into four rooms, with an annex on the southern end. It is possible that the building originally comprised the three northern rooms, the southern being slightly narrower and perhaps a later addition. The remains of brick floors survived in the two central rooms, one of which also contained a hearth, perhaps indicating that this was the living accommodation, while the other rooms would have formed the workshop, including areas for clay preparation and the storage of stock.

Figure 16 The base of the beehive kiln at Lewis's Pottery (Site 5) during excavations in 2000 showing the six fire-boxes and a single doorway behind the scale, together with the foundations for the surrounding hovel (Photo courtesy of Earthworks Archaeology).

The annex, at the southern end, contained seven rows of edge-set bricks spaced 0.15-0.20m apart, the clay deposit beneath them having been affected by heat (Figure 17). It seems likely that this structure formed part of a drying floor on which the pottery was gradually and partially dried before being transferred to the kiln for firing.

The Finds

A large quantity of pottery wasters and kiln furniture was recovered from the deposits within the pottery complex, allowing the characterization of vessel types and forms produced on the site and the means by which they were both stacked and fired. The Lewis Pottery manufactured a variety of black and brown lead-glazed vessels with a red fabric, and included large bowls and dishes, round-bodied and straight-sided mugs, storage jars and chamber pots, together with white, slip-decorated bowls, dishes, and mugs. Industrial vessels in the form of white lead extraction pots were also recovered from the site, as well as moulded architectural fragments and glazed roofing ridge tiles.

Of the more unusual ceramic items recovered was a fragment from a possible ornamental vessel with an applied moulded face of a bearded man with a high forehead and longish hair. This unusual vessel had been biscuit fired and coated in a white slip but had never reached its second, or glost, firing. Only a single example of this type was found, and it may be reasonably assumed that it was not typical of the vessel types being produced.

The kiln furniture recovered included large cylindrical saggars with pierced walls, crescent-shaped spacers, small pyramid-shaped spacers and crude pillow spacers formed by merely squeezing a piece of clay within the fist. Many examples still bear the fingerprints and nail marks of the potter.

Catalogue of selected vessels from Lewis's Pottery

1. A Jardinière (plant stand) from the excavations at Lewis Pottery. Unglazed, biscuit fired, buff fabric. 220mm diameter. From context 83; cottage floor.
2. Blackware cup. 75mm diameter. Context 66, clay deposit beneath drying floor.
3. Blackware bottle. 45mm diameter. Context 128, fill of a drain.
4. Blackware cup. 112mm diameter. Context 83, cottage floor.
5. Blackware cup/posset pot. 150mm diameter. Context 172, fill of a pit.
6. Blackware cup. 160mm diameter. Context 19, fill of a well.
7. Blackware cup. 110mm diameter. Context 128, fill of a drain.

Figure 17 The 18th-/19th-century pottery workshop and cottage at Lewis's Pottery (Site 5) during excavations in 2000 (Photo courtesy of Earthworks Archaeology).

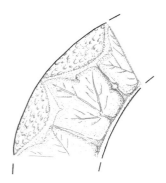

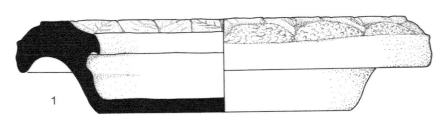

Figure 18 A Jardinière (plant stand) from the excavations at Lewis Pottery. Scale 1:2

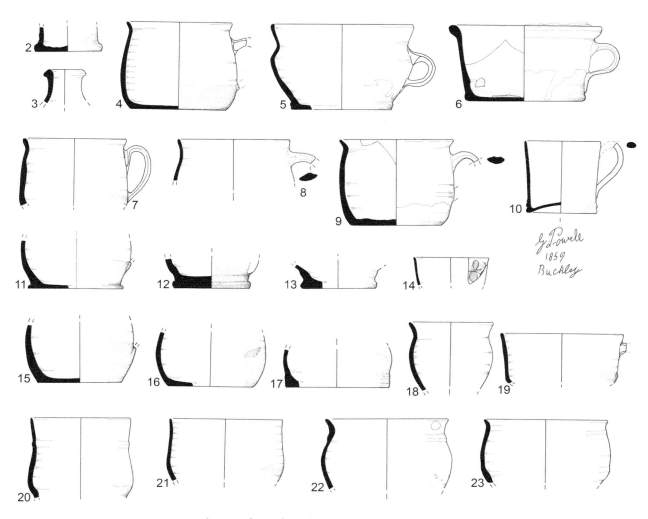

Figure 19 A selection of cups from the excavations at Lewis Pottery. Scale 1:4.

8. Blackware cup. 120mm diameter. Context 25, fill of a pit.
9. Blackware cup. 120mm diameter. Context 19, fill of well.
10. Engraved cup in unglazed, biscuit fired, buff fabric. 80mm diameter. Context 83, cottage floor.
11. Blackware cup. 100mm diameter base. Context 218, fill of a pit.
12. Blackware cup. 83mm diameter base. Context 86, wall of workshop.
13. Blackware cup. 80mm diameter base. Context 19, fill of well.
14. White salt-glazed stoneware tea bowl with scratch blue decoration. 80mm diameter. Context 86, wall of workshop.
15. Blackware cup. 88mm diameter base. Context 19, fill of well.
16. Blackware cup. 90mm diameter base. Context 19, fill of well.
17. Blackware cup. 110mm base diameter. Context 193, fill Context a drain.
18. Blackware cup. 90mm diameter. Context 30, fill of posthole in Building 1.
19. Blackware cup. 130mm diameter. Context 240, deposit.
20. Blackware cup. 105mm diameter. Context 235, deposit.
21. Blackware cup. 120mm diameter. Context 218, fill of a pit.
22. Slipware cup. 130mm diameter. Context 219, fill of a pit.
23. Blackware cup. 135mm diameter. Context 95, deposit.

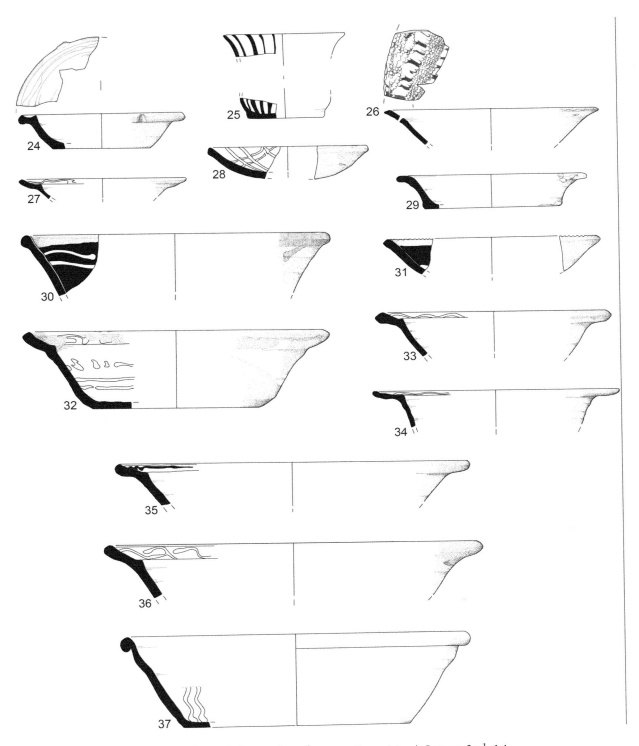

Figure 20 Slip-trailed wares from the excavations at Lewis Pottery. Scale 1:4.

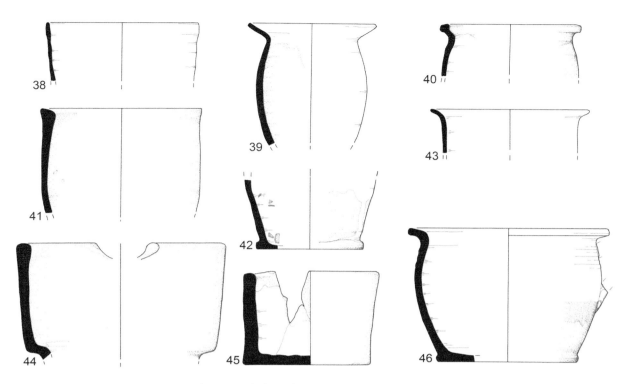

Figure 21 Medium vessels from the excavations at Lewis Pottery. Scale 1:4.

24. Slip-trailed bowl. 180mm diameter. Context 97, deposit.
25. Slip-trailed cup with buff fabric. 129mm diameter. Context 193, fill of a drain.
26. Press-moulded dish with trailed and combed slip decoration and 'pie-crust' edge. 232mm diameter. Context 44, deposit.
27. Slip-trailed bowl. 178mm diameter. Context 103, foundations of Building 2.
28. Slip-trailed, press-moulded dish. 175mm diameter. Context 84, fill to a pit.
29. Slip-trailed bowl. 200mm diameter. Context 43, deposit.
30. Slip-trailed bowl. 326mm diameter. Context 134, fill of a drain.
31. Slip-trailed, press-moulded dish. 233mm diameter. Context 134, fill of a drain.
32. Slip-trailed bowl. 323mm diameter. Context 189, fill of a drain.
33. Slip-trailed bowl. 255mm diameter. Context 103, foundations of Building 2.
34. Slip-trailed bowl. 265mm diameter. Context 191, fill of a drain.
35. Slip-trailed bowl. 375mm diameter. Context 191, fill of a drain.
36. Slip-trailed bowl. 40mm diameter. Context 97, deposit.
37. Slip-trailed bowl. 380mm diameter. Context 134, fill of a drain.
38. Blackware jar. 167mm diameter. Context 211, deposit.
39. Blackware jar. 142mm diameter. Context 237, deposit.
40. Blackware jar. 154mm diameter. Context 240, deposit.
41. Redware jar, probably intended for industrial use. 175mm diameter. Context 19, fill of well.
42. Blackware jar. 118mm diameter base. Context 191, fill of a drain.
43. Blackware jar. 173mm diameter. Context 191, fill of a drain.
44. Redware vessel probably intended for industrial use. 225mm diameter. Context 19, fill of well.
45. Blackware jar probably intended for industrial use. 143mm diameter. Context 83, cottage floor.
46. Blackware chamber pot. 212mm diameter. Context 19, fill of well.

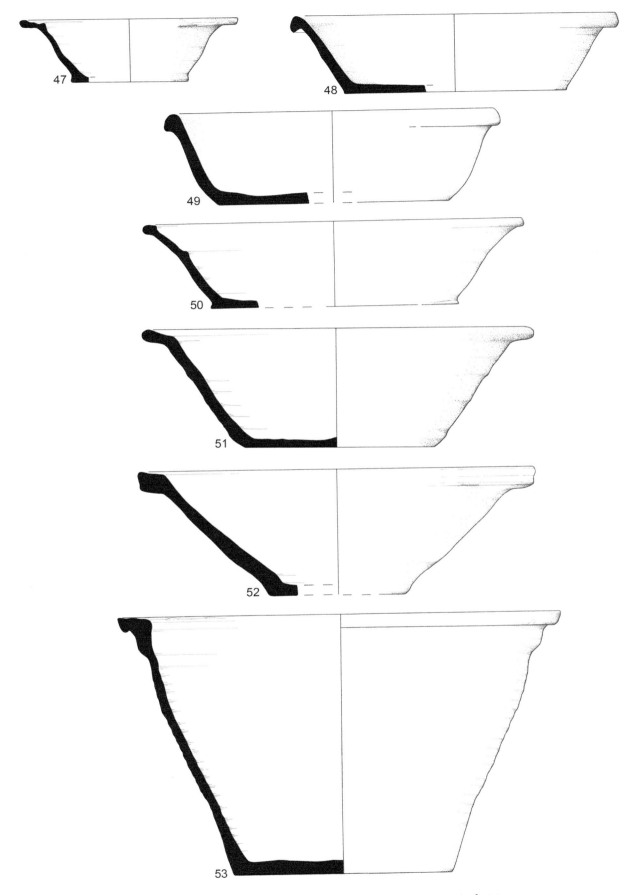

Figure 22 Large bowls from the excavations at Lewis Pottery. Scale 1:4.

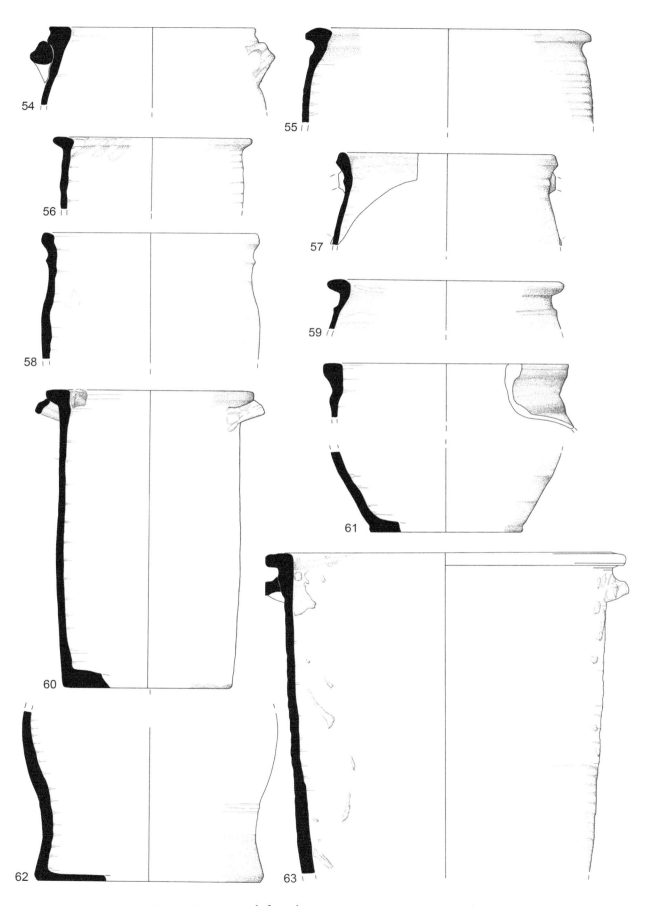

Figure 23 Large vessels from the excavations at Lewis Pottery. Scale 1:4.

47. Slip-trailed bowl. 230mm diameter. Context 191, fill of a drain.
48. Large blackware bowl. 346mm diameter. Context 93, fill of a drain.
49. Unglazed bowl with red slip wash to interior and exterior. Biscuit fired. 354mm diameter. Context 1, backfill deposit in Kiln 3 chamber.
50. Blackware dish. Glazed on interior. 400mm diameter. Context 171, fill of a pit.
51. Large blackware bowl. 420mm diameter. Context 191, fill of a drain.
52. Large blackware bowl. Glaze to interior. 420mm diameter. Context 1, backfill deposit in Kiln 3 chamber.
53. Blackware bowl. Glaze to interior. 470mm diameter. Context 1, backfill deposit in Kiln 3 chamber.
54. Blackware, lug-handled jar. Glaze to interior. 225mm diameter. Context 25, fill of a pit.
55. Blackware jar. 302mm diameter. Context 128, fill of a drain.
56. Blackware jar. 215mm diameter. Context 112, fill of a drain.
57. Handled blackware jar. 240mm diameter. Context 191, fill of a drain.
58. Blackware jar. Black glaze to interior. Heavily sooted exterior. 237mm diameter. Context 112, fill to a drain.
59. Blackware jar. 250mm diameter. Context 93, fill to a drain.
60. Tall lug-handled blackware jar. 225mm diameter. Context 169, deposit.
61. Blackware jar. 265mm diameter. Context 218, fill to a pit.
62. Blackware jar. 243mm diameter. Context 19, fill to a well.
63. Blackware, lug-handled jar with glaze to interior and exterior. 390mm diameter. Context 1, backfill deposit in Kiln 3 chamber.

Price's Pottery (Site 11), 2014-15

Sophie Watson

The site of Price's Pottery (Figure 1, 11; SJ 2757 6462) lies adjacent to the northern boundary of the grounds of Elfed School and much of it is now occupied by two modern houses. Cartographic evidence indicates that a pottery was in operation on this site by the late 18th century and continued until the late 19th century. The 1757 Lordship of Ewloe map shows two rectangular buildings, but no kiln, identifying the occupier as Charles Price, but with nothing to confirm that a pottery was then in operation. The book of reference to the Gwysaney estate map of 1781 identifies the occupier as his widow, Martha, while their son, also called Charles, appears in the Gwysaney clay accounts for 1783-93, although the 1794 entry is in the name of Martha, perhaps suggesting the son had died (Messham 1956, 34 and 56; Rutter 1977). The business continued in the family until at least 1868, when yet another Charles Price is listed as a manufacturer of earthenwares in *Slaters Trade Directory* of North Wales. The pottery had evidently closed by 1874 as it does not appear in that edition of Worral's *Trade Directory* and is not mentioned in any later trade directories. However, it is depicted on the Ordnance Survey 1st edition 25-inch (1:2500) map of 1884, which shows a single kiln and two buildings, as well as a circular feature, possibly a blunger, and a small pond, perhaps a soaking pit. The buildings on the 1884 map correspond with those depicted in 1757.

The stylised depiction of the buildings in 1757 suggests that the larger, northern building was the dwelling, while the other was the potter's workshop (Rutter 1977).

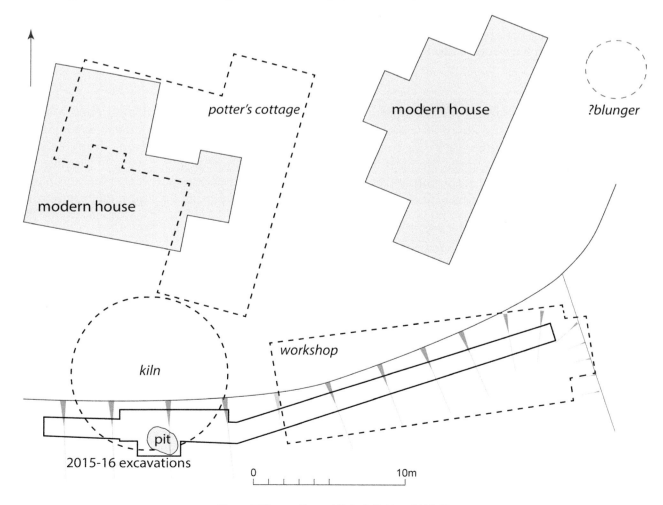

Figure 24 Excavations at Price's Pottery 2014-15.

In 1974 extensive groundworks were undertaken, terracing the area south of the pottery to level out a playing field for the school. This had a major impact on a dump of wasters immediately south and west of the pottery. Rescue investigations at that time recovered a significant quantity of 18th- to 19th-century pottery and kiln furniture, including very fine mottled ware tankards (Davey 1976a, 23), a summary report on which was produced by John Rutter (1977).

As part of a community-based project, funded by Cadw, two seasons of excavations were undertaken by CPAT in 2014-15, in association with staff and pupils from Elfed High School, and members of the local community (Hankinson and Culshaw 2014; Watson and Culshaw 2015). The excavation focused on a narrow strip along the northern boundary of the playing field, within which it was hoped to reveal part of one of the pottery buildings and also the edge of the kiln. The playing field has been terraced into the slope at this location to around 2m below the gardens on the other side of the boundary. This indicates the extent to which the land surface has been modified with the attendant loss of the archaeological material identified in 1974.

The excavations revealed little of archaeological interest relating to the structures of the pottery; the only significant feature identified was a large pit, potentially dug as a clay source but then backfilled with a range of material, including a large quantity of pottery, parts of a kiln and associated slags. Overall, the excavation did recover a significant assemblage of pottery, mainly wasters, which has added further to our knowledge of the range and date of wares produced at Price's Pottery.

It is also worth noting that a small excavation was undertaken by CPAT in 2014 in the adjacent field to the east, on behalf of Flintshire County Council (Hankinson and Jones 2014). This comprised a single trench which revealed no obvious features but yielded additional pottery fragments that were almost certainly derived from Price's Pottery and included the best examples of press-moulded slipware from the pottery site, some of which have been dated to the early 18th century.

The pottery

A total of 9,571 sherds of post-medieval pottery were recovered between 2014 and 2015, representing only a small sample of the dump of wasters which had accumulated along the southern edge of the pottery. The report by Rutter (1977) illustrated the range of pottery which was recovered from the site during the 1970s, and this forms the basis for the following section, although it was not possible to determine the whereabouts of the pottery recovered in 1974 and therefore no direct comparisons have been made. Where examples from these investigations are illustrated here, they have been redrawn, based on Rutter's illustrations.

The majority of the pottery recovered during 2014 and 2015 came from the topsoil and had evidently been redeposited during the groundworks in 1974, although the most complete vessels were found within a deep pit which was only partly excavated. Finds included some nearly complete examples of jugs, cups, flared, globular vessels with a single handle (similar to a chamber pot) and single-handled, flared bowls.

The majority of the wares were wheel-thrown, highly-fired earthenware vessels, particularly fine tablewares, including hollow-ware forms like cups, tankards, dishes, and bowls. There were also some coarser kitchen/pantry wares, including flared bowls or basins, large flared bowls or pancheons (otherwise known in Buckley as 'Pan-mugs') and chunky upright jars. Vessels similar in form to a chamber pot seem to have been produced regularly in a variety of glazes and unglazed vessels including plant pots were also found during the excavations. Very few of the larger coarseware vessels, such as cooking pots, were present within the assemblage, although they are well known from other contemporary potteries in Buckley, such as Brookhill (Site 1).

It appears that Price's Pottery were producing similar styles of vessel, in a variety of glazes, with the predominant glaze type appearing to be blackware, though there were also significant quantities of slip-trailed wares, mottled wares, brown ware and lead-glazed ware.

Small quantities of press-moulded slipware and agate-bodied ware were also present, as well as a few individual sherds identified as yellow ware and sgraffito.

As might be expected from a dump of wasters, there were also large quantities of saggars and other kiln furniture, including stilts, separators, the remains of a kiln shelf, bricks, and firing waste.

Identification of form

Owing to the overall size of the pottery assemblage recovered, its general lack of stratified provenance and the resources available for its study, it was necessary to employ a method of selective analysis that allowed the most useful information to be extracted, rather than studying the whole assemblage in detail. Therefore, the more distinctive sherds, such as bases and rims, were examined more thoroughly as these were more likely to give an indication of dimension and form for the individual vessels being produced. Unless a body sherd displayed distinct characteristics of a certain vessel form, indistinct body sherds were generally grouped together according to glaze type as it would be otherwise impossible to determine the exact vessel from which it derived. Body sherds equated to 62% of the overall assemblage.

Table 3 Summary quantification of pottery recovered from Price's Pottery in 2015-16

Type of ware	No. of sherds	%
Black-ware	5519	58
Slip-trailed	1067	11
Unglazed	1011	11
Mottled ware	917	10
Overfired	419	4
Brown ware	289	3
Lead-glazed	283	3
Press-moulded	54	<1
Agate	8	<1
Yellow-ware	2	<1
Chocolate-dipped	1	<1
Sgrafitto	1	<1
Total	9571	

The pottery was washed and sorted by students from Elfed High School and volunteers at CPAT, initially sorting according to glaze and fabric, with further subdivisions according to the type of sherd (i.e. handle, rim, base or body). With the assistance of Christine Longworth and members of the Buckley Society, an initial system of identification was then employed using John Rutter's report (1977) as a reference guide, which enabled vessels to be grouped by their most likely form.

Blackware

Of the pottery recovered during the 2014-15 excavations, blackware was predominant, accounting for 5519 sherds and equating to over half (57%) of the overall assemblage. There are a number of variations within the blackware, although most have a red slip applied beneath the glaze. A small quantity of the blackware sherds had a more iridescent, mirror-like glaze, a style that did not appear in Buckley until the 1850s.

Vessels were either glazed all over or dripping down towards the base on the exterior. The majority of sherds from Price's Pottery display a fabric of 'laminated clay', which fires a mixture of red and buff clay, although the percentage of red clay was much higher than that of buff. Using mixed clays like this can leave a variegated surface to the pot (a method which was intended in agate-bodied wares), though the use of red slip beneath the black glaze would have tempered this appearance and would have created a much richer 'black'.

The majority of the blackware comprised a range of thrown, highly-fired, fine-bodied open wares. However, owing to the often-small size of the sherds, it has not always been possible to determine with confidence the exact type of vessel, or what its function may have been. Vessels are therefore discussed in general terms of form, with only a suggestion being made as to their possible function unless this is known with certainty.

Drinking vessels

Based on comparisons to other similar vessels, 761 sherds of blackware are assumed to have come from small, fineware vessels, probably drinking vessels such as cups and tankards. Of the 761, only 37 were assumed to have come from tankards.

Although there were variations in the style and size of the vessels, there appear to have been some distinct forms that were being produced regularly and these are consistent with the examples illustrated by Rutter. Variations of necked or flared cups with a pronounced footring were common [nos. 1-11], as well as straighter-sided vessels with a simple base (nos. 13-24).

In most cases, the bases of the vessels were fairly wide, on average around 100mm in diameter, but a range of more delicate cups were also being produced (nos. 3-4), with much smaller bases of around 45mm in diameter (most of which were identified by Rutter). The rims on these drinking vessels appear to have been relatively simple and straight or slightly out-turned.

The 'necked cup' appears to have been most regularly produced at Prices, with 262 of the blackware sherds being allocated this form (nos. 1 and 5). Around 98 sherds were identified as simpler, straighter sided cups with a slightly angled base (nos. 14-23).

Narrow-necked vessels (bottles, jugs or jars)

Eleven slightly thickened, upright rim sherds (nos. 29-33) with diameters of 40-80mm are likely to have come from either bottles, jugs or jars. One vessel recovered from the excavation which is likely to have had a rim like this was a near complete example of a bottle or cider jar, although this was unfortunately missing the rim (no. 34).

Jugs

Rutter identified a fine blackware jug or urinal, with a pronounced footring at the base and a diameter of 150mm (no. 36). The recent excavations produced an example of a near complete blackware jug. This was a medium-sized, pear-shaped vessel, with an out-turned rim, 100mm in diameter. Attachments for a single handle were visible below the rim and a pronounced footring at the base (no. 35). Other black-glazed vessels similar to this form were also identified, though most were of slightly larger dimensions (nos. 36-41).

In addition, vessels similar in form to some of the blackware cups, with the more simple, angled base were present (nos. 46 and 48-50), though of larger dimensions. It is possible that these two represent the base of another form of jug or perhaps a jar.

Straight-sided, single-handled vessels

Several straight-sided vessels with a single handle were identified within the blackware assemblage (see Figure 26, 42-45), with a diameter of around 160mm at the base and a handle positioned just above the footring. Two vessels of similar form were identified by Rutter. It is possible that these are a form of the Buckley 'dip pot' often used during milking or transferring milk from one pot to another.

Flared, single-handled vessels

Similar to the straight-sided, single-handled vessels discussed above, several rim sherds were identified which had flared sides. Remnants of a handle could be seen extending just below a rolled rim. These were of relatively fine fabric, with rim diameters measuring around 220mm (nos. 63-64). Vessels of similar form are often referred to as 'stool pans'.

Single-handled, globular jars

A number of vessels with everted or hooked rims were identified, in varying styles, accounting for around 7% of the blackware. The rims typically ranged between 200-300mm in diameter, in a relatively fine fabric, with a round or globular body and a single, looped handle extending out below the rim (nos. 52-58). The functional term often attributed to this style of pot is the 'chamber pot', although it is impossible to know the exact function of these vessels which appear at Price's and they could equally have been what was known as a bushel pan or measure.

A similar, near complete mottled ware example (no. 112) was also identified at Prices and parallels also appear in the brown ware and elsewhere in Buckley, at Brookhill (Site 1), Pinfold Land (Site 19) and Hancock's Pottery (Site 14), with black, mottled and slip-trailed glazes.

Straight-sided vessels

A total of 71 blackware base sherds represented straight-sided or inverted-sided vessels the bases ranging between 180mm and 260mm in diameter. These were also of relatively fine fabric and possibly represent a form of storage jar (no. 47). Similar blackware examples have been found at Hancock's Pottery (Site 14), which was operational between c.1790 and 1886.

Shallow bowls

Several examples of shallow blackware bowls were recovered, having characteristically wide, everted rims with a rounded body profile below. The vessels were typically 190mm in diameter and 30mm high (see Figure 27, 59).

Flared-base vessels

The blackware assemblage included examples of base sherds with a flared body, although unfortunately no surviving rims. The vessels measured between 130mm and 140mm in diameter and could be from a variety of vessels, such as bowls, jugs or jars (no. 50).

Larger blackwares

The larger blackware vessels appear to fall into two main categories, being either large, flared bowls (nos. 65-75) or large cylindrical jars (nos. 76-82). These were usually only glazed internally, as well as the rim and are often referred to as pancheons or 'pan mugs' in Buckley. A total of 52 blackware sherds were assigned to this category, of which ten were base sherds and the remainder rims.

The large, flared bowls display a wide everted rim in a range of styles, often with an indentation around the edge of the rim. These rims vary between 370mm and 560mm in diameter.

The rims of the more cylindrical vessels ranged in size between 240mm and 400mm in diameter with predominantly rolled, thickened rims (see Figure 28, 76), or collared rims (nos. 79-82), although examples of squared rims (no. 77), and flanged rims (no. 78) were also identified.

The base sherds likely to correspond to some of these larger vessels (nos. 72-75) are typically very plain in their form.

Catalogue of blackware

1. Blackware vessel with an out-turned rim and angled footring. Found in 1974 and recorded as Rutter Type 18. Glaze to interior and exterior, terminating just above the base. Red earthenware fabric. Diameter 105mm.

2. Blackware base with angled footring, found in 1974 and recorded as Rutter Type 19. Glaze to interior and exterior, terminating just above the base. Red slip wash visible beneath the glaze. Red earthenware fabric. 100mm diameter base.

3. Blackware base sherd with narrow, splayed footring (Rutter Type 19). Body flares outwards from base. All over glaze. Red earthenware fabric. 70mm diameter base.

4. Blackware base sherd, probably from a flared cup, with deep/slightly splayed footring (Rutter Type 20). Fine, out-turned rim fragment adhered to interior of base where collapsed. Flared, rounded vessel profile. All over glaze, terminating 30mm above base on exterior with red under-slip, terminating 15mm above base. Red earthenware fabric. 80mm diameter base.

5. Blackware flared cup with iridescent glaze. Narrow, rounded footring and visible handle stub. All over glaze, terminating 14mm above base on exterior. Red earthenware fabric. 80mm diameter base.

6. Blackware base sherd with footring. Glaze to interior and exterior. Red earthenware fabric. 90mm diameter base.

7. Blackware base sherd with splayed footring. Vessel body flares outwards above base. All over glaze, dribbled to footring on exterior. Red earthenware body. 100mm diameter base.

8. Blackware base sherd with narrow rounded footring. Vessel body flares slightly outwards from base then turns inwards around 20mm above base. All over glaze, dribbled to around 23mm above base on exterior. Red earthenware fabric. 80mm diameter base.

9. Blackware base sherd with rounded footring. Rounded vessel profile, flaring outwards from base. Visible handle stub. All over glaze, dribbled to around 18mm above base on exterior. Red earthenware fabric. 90mm diameter base.

10. Blackware base sherd with footring. Body flares outwards above the base. All over glaze, dribbled to around 18mm above base on exterior. Red earthenware fabric. 90mm diameter base.

11. Very fine blackware base sherd with footring. Glaze visible to interior, red slip wash visible on exterior. Vessel body flares sharply outwards above the base. Red earthenware fabric. 60mm diameter base.

12. Fine blackware tankard base sherd with squared footring. All over glaze terminating around 14mm above the footring. Red earthenware fabric. 70mm diameter base.

13. Blackware base sherd with rounded base, narrowing towards to top half of the vessel. Black glaze to interior and partially to exterior. Red earthenware fabric. 73mm diameter base.

14. Blackware base sherd from a probable cup with iridescent glaze. Angled base leading into a straight-sided vessel. All over glaze, terminating 20mm above the base on exterior. Red earthenware fabric. 90mm diameter base.

15. Blackware base sherd found in 1974 and recorded as Rutter Type 23. Plain, rounded base. All over glaze, dripped down towards base on exterior. Visible handle stub. Red earthenware fabric. 105mm diameter base.

16. Blackware base sherd with iridescent glaze (Rutter Type 23). Straight-sided vessel profile. All over glaze, dribbled to around 24mm above base on exterior with red under-slip. Red earthenware fabric. 100mm diameter base.

17. Blackware, plain base sherd from a probable cup or mug (Rutter Type 23). Flares outwards slightly from base then straight-sided. Handle stub visible. All over glaze, terminating 20mm above base with red under-slip, terminating 7mm above base. Red earthenware fabric. 110mm diameter base.

18. Blackware, plain base sherd from a probable cup with handle stub. Vessel body flares very slightly outwards from base. All over glaze, terminating 32mm above base on exterior. Red earthenware fabric. 120mm diameter base.

19. Dark brown/black iridescent glazed base sherd. Plain, rounded base (Rutter Type 23). Straight-sided vessel. All over glaze, terminating 23mm above base on exterior. Red earthenware fabric. 100mm diameter base.

20. Blackware, plain, base sherd (Rutter Type 24). Flares outwards from base for 15mm then straight sided. All over glaze terminating 27mm above base with red under-slip. Red earthenware fabric. 110mm diameter base.

21. Blackware, slightly out-turned rim sherd. Partial handle surviving. All over glaze. Red earthenware fabric. 120mm diameter.

22. Fine blackware base sherd from a probable cup with double line of reeding visible on exterior, just above the base. Black all-over glaze terminating 7mm above base. Red earthenware fabric. 120mm base diameter.

23. Blackware base sherd with iridescent glaze. Plain base, flaring outwards before straightening out 10mm above base. All-over glaze, terminating 10mm above base at change in angle. Red earthenware fabric. 140mm diameter base.

24. Blackware, out-turned rim sherd. Straight sided vessel profile. All over glaze. Red earthenware fabric. 120mm diameter.

25. Blackware handle measuring 21mm wide. Red earthenware fabric.

26. Very fine black-glazed handle measuring 16mm wide. Vessel appears to be a necked cup – no rim diameter available. Red earthenware fabric.

27. Fine blackware handle measuring 18mm wide. Glaze is iridescent. Vessel is probably a straight-sided cup or mug with a diameter of 140mm and an out-turned rim. Red earthenware fabric.

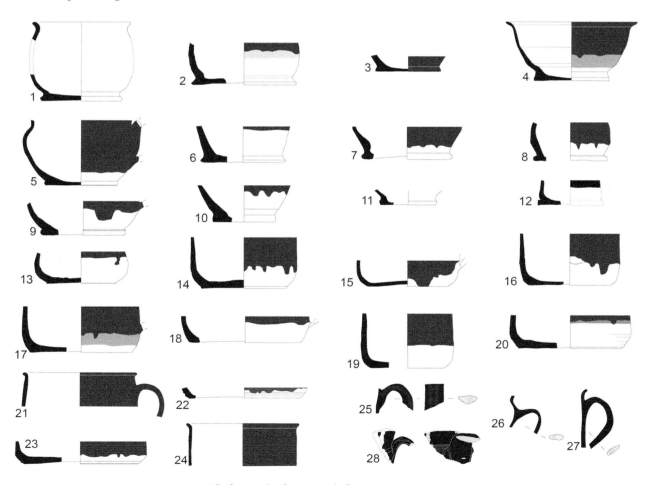

Figure 25 Blackware drinking vessels from Price's Pottery. Scale 1:4.

28. Black-glazed iridescent handle fragment measuring 30mm wide. Reeding visible on vessel body where handle adjoins. Red earthenware fabric. Probable large vessel.

29. Fine, blackware upright rim from a bottle/jar. All-over black iridescent glaze. Red earthenware fabric. 45mm diameter.

30. Fine, blackware rolled, upright rim from a bottle/jar. All-over black iridescent glaze. Red earthenware fabric. 60mm diameter.

31. Fine, blackware rolled, upright rim from a bottle/jar. All-over black iridescent glaze. Red earthenware fabric. 50mm diameter.

32. Fine, blackware upright rim from a bottle/jar. All-over black iridescent glaze. Red earthenware fabric. 80mm diameter.

33. Fine, blackware upright rim from a bottle/jar. Flares sharply outwards 18mm below rim. All-over black iridescent glaze. Red earthenware fabric. 45mm diameter.

34. Near complete blackware cider jar. Glaze is all over and iridescent, stopping around 25mm above the base on the exterior. Red earthenware fabric. Vessel measures around 160mm tall and 115mm in diameter at the base.

35. Fine, blackware, medium-sized, pear-shaped jug. Near complete. Black glaze to interior and exterior terminating 36mm above the base. Red slip wash visible on exterior below the black glaze and forming part of the external decoration. Slip wash terminates 27mm above the base. Stub for adjoining handle visible. Red earthenware fabric. 100mm diameter.

36. Fine, blackware jug or urinal found in 1974 and identified by Rutter. Black glaze to interior and exterior. Red earthenware fabric. 150mm diameter base.

37. Blackware base sherd from a possible jug with deep straight-sided footring. Rounded profile, the body flaring outwards above base. Glaze to interior, but none visible to exterior, though red slip wash visible 30mm above base. Red earthenware fabric. 90mm diameter base.

38. Blackware base sherd from possible jug with iridescent glaze and pronounced angular footring. Upright vessel with slightly convex sides. Red earthenware fabric with small percentage of buff clay. 140mm diameter base.

39. Blackware base sherd from possible jug with deep, angular footring. Vessel body flares outwards above base. All over glaze, terminating 18mm above base on exterior. Red earthenware fabric. 120mm diameter base.

40. Blackware base sherd from straight-sided, single-handled jug with rounded footring similar to examples found in 1974. All-over glaze stopping around 18mm above footring on exterior. Red under-slip beneath glaze. Red earthenware fabric. 160mm diameter base.

41. Blackware base sherd from possible straight-sided, single-handled jug with footring found in 1974 and identified by Rutter. A handle stub protrudes from just above the base. Black glaze to interior and exterior, terminating just above the base. Red earthenware fabric. 160mm diameter base.

42. Blackware base sherd with squared and slightly up-turned footring. All-over glaze stopping around 18mm above footring on exterior. Red under-slip beneath glaze. Vessel is relatively straight sided with evidence of handle stub extending just above the base. Red earthenware fabric. 180mm diameter base.

43. Fine blackware base sherd, probably from a jug. All over glaze with red under slip, stopping around 10mm above footring on exterior. Vessel is upright with the remains of handle stub and squared footring. Red earthenware fabric. 160mm diameter base.

44. Fine blackware base sherd from a possible storage jar. An upright vessel with slightly inverted sides and squared footring. Black glaze to interior and on exterior to footring. Red earthenware fabric. 190mm diameter base.

45. Blackware base sherd from a straight-sided vessel with angular footring. Full glaze, terminating 25mm above the base. Red earthenware fabric. 180mm diameter base.

46. Overfired blackware vessel, possibly a jug, with a splayed base. Black glaze to interior and exterior, terminating 15mm above the base on exterior. Red earthenware fabric. 120mm diameter base.

47. Blackware base sherd with squared footring. All-over glaze, stopping around 20mm above footring on exterior. Red under-slip. Red earthenware fabric. 250mm diameter base.
48. Blackware base sherd with iridescent glaze. Plain base with slightly rounded vessel profile. Red earthenware fabric. 120mm diameter base.
49. Blackware base sherd with iridescent glaze. Straight base with flaring vessel walls above. Red earthenware fabric. 140mm diameter base.
50. Blackware base sherd with pronounced angled footring. Glaze to interior only. Red slip wash to exterior. Red earthenware fabric. 140mm diameter (though also 160mm variations). Similar to examples recorded by Rutter.
51. Fine blackware bowl or jar with angular base. Glaze is iridescent and only visible on interior. Red slip wash to exterior. Red earthenware fabric. 140mm diameter base.

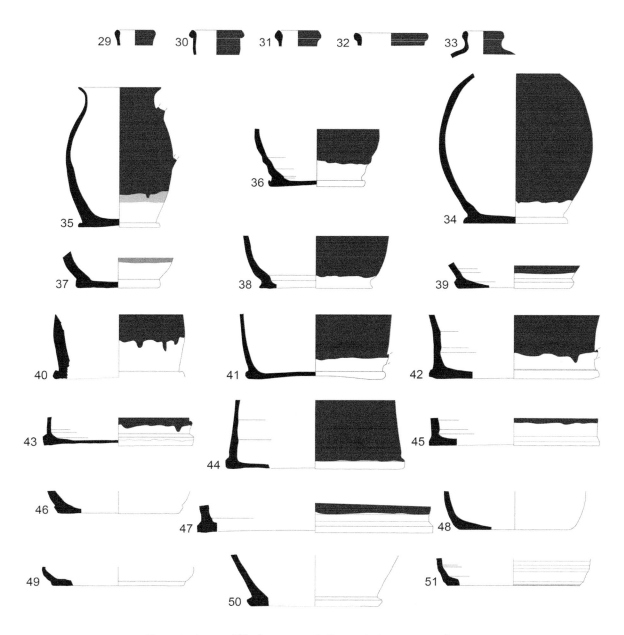

Figure 26 Assorted blackware vessels from Price's Pottery. Scale 1:4.

52. Blackware hooked rim. Black iridescent all over glaze. Red earthenware fabric. 140mm diameter.

53. Blackware everted rim sherd from a probably chamber pot with partial handle remaining. All over glaze. Red earthenware fabric. 200mm diameter.

54. Blackware, everted rim sherd. Vessel flares slightly below the rim. All over glaze. Red earthenware fabric. 200mm diameter. There are similar vessels to this with 210mm diameter.

55. Very fine blackware hooked rim sherd. Glazed all-over. Red earthenware fabric. 220mm diameter.

56. Blackware flat everted rim. Iridescent all over glaze. Red earthenware fabric. 220mm diameter.

57. Blackware everted rim sherd. Vessel walls flare below the rim. All over iridescent glaze. Red earthenware fabric. 200mm diameter.

58. Blackware everted rim sherd with reeding below. Vessel flares out below the rim. Degraded rim sherd. Red earthenware fabric. 220mm rim diameter.

59. Blackware rim sherd. Glaze to interior and rim, red slip wash to exterior. Everted rim measuring 23mm wide. Red earthenware fabric. 190mm diameter.

60. Blackware storage vessel or mixing bowl with thickened rim with one band of reeding towards the middle of the vessel. Glaze is iridescent. Red earthenware fabric. 150mm rim diameter.

61. Blackware rolled rim of a flared bowl or basin. Black iridescent all over glaze. Red earthenware fabric. 180mm diameter.

62. Blackware, thickened rim from a storage vessel or mixing bowl with two bands of reeding towards the middle of the vessel. Glaze is iridescent. Red earthenware fabric. 220mm rim diameter.

63. Blackware single-handled flared bowl with a rolled rim and handle stub. Black iridescent all over glaze. Handle stub visible below rim. Red earthenware fabric. 220mm diameter.

64. Blackware single-handled flared bowl with rolled rim and single handle. Glaze is iridescent and all over. Red earthenware fabric. 220mm diameter.

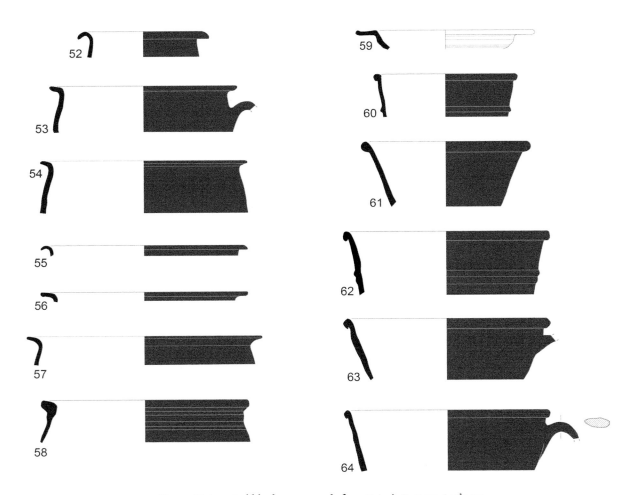

Figure 27 Assorted blackware vessels from Price's Pottery. Scale 1:4.

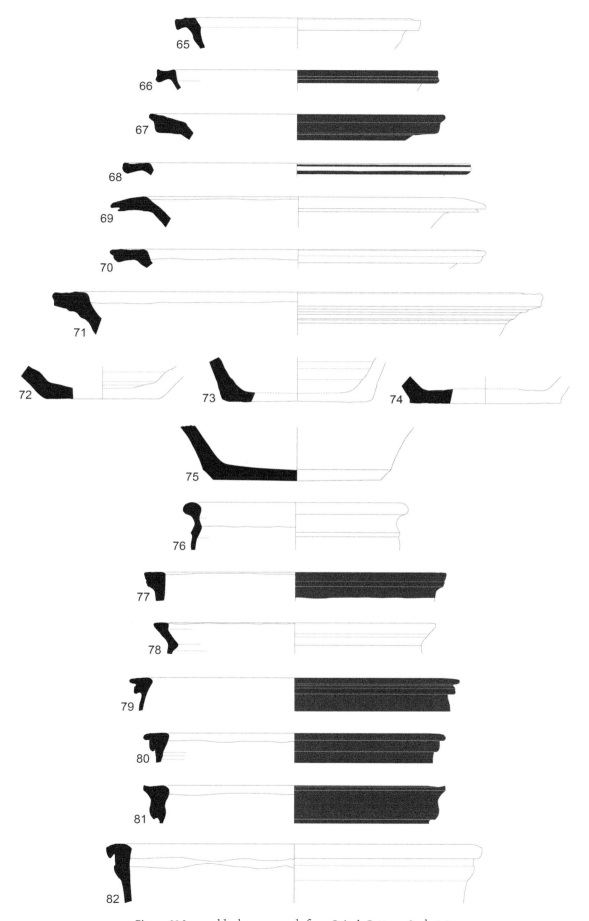

Figure 28 Larger blackware vessels from Price's Pottery. Scale 1:4.

65. Blackware pancheon with everted rim. Glaze to interior, red slip wash to exterior. Red earthenware fabric. 260mm diameter.

66. Blackware pancheon with everted and indented rim. Glaze to interior and rim. Overfired vessel. Red earthenware fabric. 300mm diameter.

67. Blackware pancheon with everted and indented rim. Glaze interior and rim, with red slip wash to exterior. Red earthenware fabric. 320mm diameter.

68. Blackware pancheon with everted rim. Glaze to interior and partially glazed rim. Red earthenware fabric. 370mm diameter.

69. Blackware pancheon with everted and indented rim. Glazed interior and red slip washed exterior. Red earthenware fabric. 400mm diameter.

70. Blackware pancheon with everted and indented rim. Glazed interior, red slip washed exterior. Red earthenware fabric. 400mm diameter (also similar variants of 350mm and 420mm diameters).

71. Blackware pancheon with everted and indented rim. Glazed interior with red slip wash to exterior. Red earthenware fabric. 560mm diameter.

72. Blackware plain base sherd. Black iridescent glaze to interior. No visible glaze to exterior. Red earthenware with small quantity of buff clay mixed in. Possibly hand wedged. 120mm diameter base.

73. Blackware plain base. Glaze to interior, red slip wash to exterior. Red earthenware mixed with small quantity of buff clay. 160mm diameter base.

74. Blackware plain base. Glaze to interior, red slip wash to exterior. Red earthenware mixed with small quantity of buff clay. 160mm diameter base.

75. Blackware angled base, found in 1974 and identified by Rutter. Glaze only visible on internal. Red earthenware fabric. 190mm diameter base.

76. Blackware upright vessel with glaze to interior, stopping 27mm below the rim. Unusual thickened, rounded rim with ribbing below. Red earthenware fabric. 240mm diameter.

77. Blackware upright vessel with glaze to interior and exterior. Partially glazed squared and indented rim. Red earthenware fabric. 320mm diameter.

78. Blackware vessel with glazed interior, red slip wash to exterior. Unusual rim-form, everted and slightly flanged. Red earthenware fabric. 300mm diameter.

79. Blackware upright vessel with all over, iridescent glaze/partially glazed rim. Ribbed and collared rim form. Red earthenware fabric. 350mm diameter.

80. Blackware upright vessel with iridescent glaze to interior and exterior. Collared rim, similar to 79. Red earthenware fabric. 320mm in diameter.

81. Blackware upright vessel with iridescent glaze to interior and exterior. Unusual collared rim. Red earthenware fabric. 320mm diameter.

82. Blackware upright vessel with glaze to interior with red underslip. No external glaze. Collared and ribbed rim. Red earthenware fabric. 400mm diameter.

Mottled Ware

Two types of mottled ware appear to have been produced at Price's Pottery, comprising a pale, and a dark variety. In the paler wares, the mottled glaze was applied to either a buff body or a red body with a buff slip coating. The darker wares occur where the mottled glaze was applied directly onto a red bodied vessel or over a red slip wash. The predominant vessel types appear to have been fineware drinking vessels, including tankards, mugs and cups.

Pale mottled wares

Drinking vessels

A total of 367 sherds were tentatively identified as cups, with base forms following the style of vessels previously identified by Rutter (nos. 93 and 97). These examples had either a slight or more pronounced foot ring. Flared cups appear to have been popular (no. 99) and one, near-complete, straight-sided mug was also identified (no. 94).

Tankards accounted for 258 sherds, typically vessels around 150mm high with plain, upright rims between 70mm-90mm in diameter (nos. 83-92, 95, 96, 98). Most displayed a foot ring in varying styles and reeding or fine ridges around the vessel body at mid-height. Although predominantly of pale, red earthenware fabric, in many cases a buff slip had been applied beneath the glaze to ensure a pale mottled finish, following the more desirable London mottled ware styles which were very pale.

Occasional buff-bodied examples also appear to have been manufactured at Price's, although these are said to have been much more expensive for the potteries to produce. Using a buff slip over a red body, as many of the Price's examples show, would give the appearance of a higher quality vessel but was actually much cheaper to produce. Only 45 of the tankard sherds identified were of a buff fabric.

Around 100 fine mottled ware handles were found during the excavations which are likely to have originated from fine mottled ware drinking vessels.

Dishes/bowls

Other pale mottled ware forms being produced at Price's included a range of around 20 dishes or bowls, with everted rims between 150mm and 250mm in diameter (see Figure 29, *100, 102*). Straight-sided vessels, possibly a variety of bowl (no. 105), measuring around 160mm at the base were also identified and were similar in form to examples seen within the black and brown wares.

Single-handled, globular jars

Forty-one of the pale mottled ware sherds were considered to have come from vessels similar in form to a chamber pot (no. 106), along with a fine, everted rim of around 250mm diameter (no. 104), although this could also have originated from an upright jar. A possible fine, necked jar with a plain out-turned rim (no. 99) was also identified within the paler mottled wares.

Catalogue of pale mottled ware

83. Pale mottled ware tankard base with buff underslip found in 1974. Footring at the base. Red earthenware fabric. 74mm diameter base.
84. Overfired mottled ware tankard with buff underslip. Fairly straight sided vessel, bulging slightly towards top and with eight bands of decorative reeding visible. Handle stub surviving. Rounded footring. All over glaze with buff under-slip over red earthenware fabric. 80mm diameter base.
85. Pale mottled ware tankard base with buff underslip found in 1974. Footring at the base and seven bands of decorative reeding around the middle of the vessel. Red earthenware fabric. 75mm diameter base.
86. Pale mottled ware tankard with angled footring and single line of reeding immediately above. All over glaze, dribbled to just above the base on exterior with buff under-slip beneath. Straight sided vessel with four visible bands of decorative reeding to upper half of vessel walls. Red earthenware fabric. 80mm diameter base.
87. Pale, buff bodied mottled ware tankard base found by Rutter in 1974. Footring at the base and four bands of decorative reeding visible around the middle of the vessel. Buff fabric. 83mm base diameter.
88. Mottled ware base sherd with slightly splayed footring. All over glaze, dribbled towards base on exterior with red under-slip. Red earthenware fabric. 90mm diameter base. Possible cup or mug base.
89. Pale mottled ware base sherd with splayed footring. All over glaze with buff under-slip, terminating above the base on exterior. Red earthenware fabric. 80mm diameter base.
90. Pale mottled ware tankard base with buff underslip found in 1974. Two visible bands of decorative reeding on the body of the vessel and footring at the base. Red earthenware fabric. 72mm diameter base.

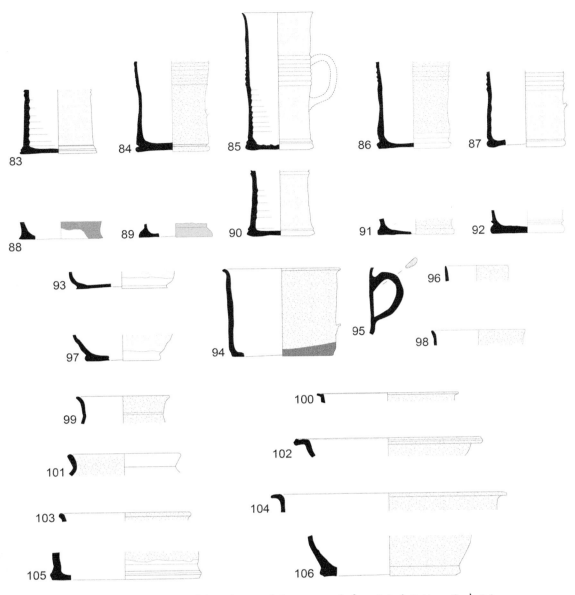

Figure 29 Examples of the paler mottled ware vessels from Price's Pottery. Scale 1:4.

91. Mottled ware probable tankard base sherd with squared footring. Red earthenware fabric. 80mm diameter base.
92. Pale, mottled ware tankard base with rounded footring and reeding above. Straight sided vessel. Pale red earthenware fabric. 80mm diameter base.
93. Pale, mottled ware probable cup base sherd with buff underslip found in 1974. Slightly angled footring. Red earthenware fabric. 98mm diameter base.
94. Near complete pale mottled ware cup or mug with buff underslip. Handle stub visible. Glazed to the base with a darker band around the base where the glaze has settled more heavily. Red earthenware fabric. 105mm diameter base.
95. Mottled ware handle from a straight-sided cup or mug. Red earthenware with buff slip-wash over. Vessel is 120mm wide.
96. Fine pale mottled ware probable tankard rim. Plain, upright rim with all over glaze and buff underslip. Red earthenware fabric. 70mm diameter.
97. Pale mottled ware probable cup base with buff underslip found in 1974. Rounded footring. Red earthenware fabric. 80mm diameter base.
98. Pale mottled ware mug or tankard rim sherd, slightly out-turned. Straight-sided vessel with all over glaze and buff under-slip. Red earthenware fabric. 100mm diameter.

99. Fine pale mottled ware rim sherd from a possible jar. Out-turned rim with body flaring towards base of vessel. All-over mottled glaze over a buff slip. Red earthenware fabric. 100mm diameter.

100. Fine, pale mottled ware possible bowl with everted rim. All-over glaze with buff under-slip. Red earthenware fabric. 150mm diameter.

101. Fine, pale mottled ware probable jar rim sherd with buff underslip. Glaze to interior up to the rim. Red slip-wash to exterior. Red earthenware fabric. 120mm diameter.

102. Pale mottled ware flared bowl rim sherd. Everted rim with mottled glaze over a buff underslip. Red earthenware fabric. 200mm diameter.

103. Fine mottled ware flared bowl or jar rim sherd with buff underslip. Rolled rim. Red earthenware fabric. 140mm diameter.

104. Fine, pale mottled ware storage jar or chamber pot with everted rim. All over glaze with buff underslip. Red earthenware fabric. 250mm diameter.

105. Pale mottled ware storage jar or large jug base sherd with angular footring. Robust, straight-sided vessel. All-over glaze, terminating 21mm above the base. Buff under-slip. Red earthenware fabric. 160mm diameter base.

106. Pale mottled ware possible chamber pot base sherd with angled footring and flared body. All over glaze with buff under-slip. Red earthenware fabric. 150mm diameter base.

Dark mottled wares

A range of slightly darker mottled ware vessels were also being produced at Price's Pottery and this appears to have been particularly adopted for the larger mottled ware vessels. Glazing directly onto the red earthenware fabric or a dark red slip produced a darker mottled ware finish.

Fine ware flared vessel

A fine rim sherd from a vessel with a flared neck was identified within the darker mottled wares. However, the limited extent of the sherd meant that a firm conclusion as to its purpose is not possible, though it may have originated from a bowl, jar, or jug (no. 113).

Single-handled, globular jars

Amongst the darker mottled ware rim sherds, a 'hooked, everted rim' appears to have been consistently produced (nos. 107-112), of which 22 examples were recorded. Vessels with this characteristic ranged between 140mm and 240mm in diameter. One near complete vessel with these attributes was recorded, which is thought to have been a chamber pot. The mottled glaze was applied over a red slip wash on a red earthenware fabric and the vessel measured 156mm high and 235mm in diameter with a hooked rim, a single looped handle and a rounded footring at the base. Additional base sherds with these characteristics were found with a dark mottled glaze (no. 118), possibly from a similar type of vessel. Other examples of mottled ware chamber pots have also been found elsewhere in Buckley at Pinfold Lane and Brookhill.

Larger wares

Two rim sherds from large storage jars (nos. 114 and 122-123) were identified with a dark mottled glaze, as well as five rim sherds from large flared bowls (nos. 121-122). Similar forms were also seen amongst the black, brown and slip-trailed wares.

Straight-sided vessels

Of the larger vessels there were several variations of straight-sided vessels, identified only from base sherds. These ranged between 120mm and 180mm in diameter and most of which displayed a slight foot ring (nos. 115-117), whilst others were relatively plain (no. 119). Some slightly flared vessels with foot rings were also apparent (no. 120), which could be large jugs or jars.

Catalogue of dark mottled ware

107. Dark mottled ware, hooked rim sherd. All-over glaze. Red earthenware fabric. 160mm diameter.

108. Very fine, dark mottled ware hooked rim sherd. Vessel wall flares out below the rim. All over glaze. Red earthenware fabric. 160mm diameter.

109. Fine, dark mottled ware, hooked rim sherd with reeding 35mm below the rim, at which point the vessel walls flare outwards and then back in towards the base. All over glaze. Red earthenware fabric. 180mm diameter.

110. Dark mottled ware curled rim. All-over glaze. Signs of reeding to exterior. Red earthenware fabric. 190mm diameter.

111. Dark mottled ware semi-rolled rim. Red earthenware fabric. 220mm dimeter.

112. Near complete, probable chamber pot with dark mottled glaze and a hooked rim. All over glaze, dribbled on exterior and terminating around 40mm above the base. Red slip-wash beneath dribbled to around 25mm above base. Rounded footring and single handle. Red earthenware fabric. 235mm diameter.

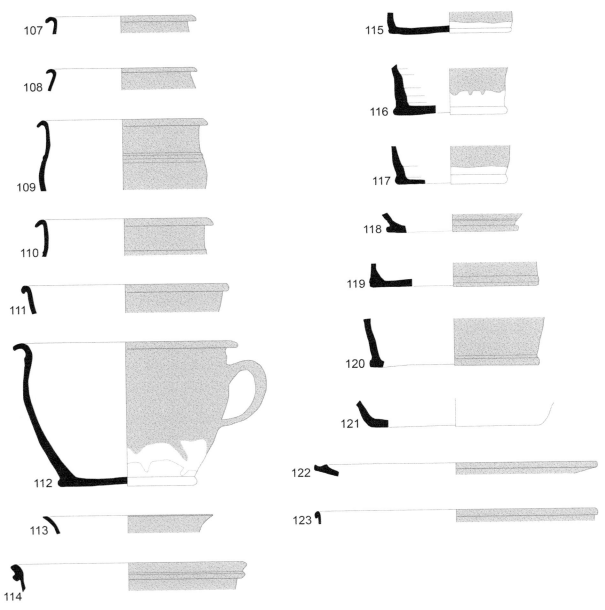

Figure 30 Examples of the dark mottled ware forms from Price's Pottery. Scale 1:4.

113. Fine, overfired mottled ware rim sherd. All over glaze. Red earthenware fabric. 180mm diameter.
114. Mottled ware collared rim sherd. All over glaze. Red earthenware fabric. 250mm rim diameter.
115. Dark mottled ware base sherd with slight rounded footring. Vessel is fairly straight-sided. Fully glazed, terminating 30mm above base on exterior. Red slip wash visible below. Red earthenware fabric mixed with a small percentage of buff clay. 120mm diameter.
116. Dark mottled ware base sherd with slight rounded footring. Fairly straight sided vessel. Full glaze, terminating 18mm above base on exterior. Red earthenware fabric. 120mm diameter base.
117. Mottled ware base sherd with slight rounded footring. Fairly straight sided vessel. Glaze to interior, red slip wash to exterior. Red earthenware fabric mixed with small percentage of buff clay. 130mm diameter base.
118. Dark mottled ware base sherd with a rounded footring and evidence of reeding above. All-over glaze. Red earthenware fabric. 140mm diameter base.
119. Dark mottled ware plain base sherd. Straight-sided vessel. Fully glazed to base. Red earthenware fabric with small percentage of buff clay. 180mm diameter base.
120. Dark mottled ware base sherd with slight rounded footring. Vessel is fairly straight-sided. Fully glazed, terminating 30mm above base on exterior. Red slip wash visible below. Red earthenware fabric mixed with a small percentage of buff clay. 120mm diameter base.
121. Mottled ware, plain base sherd. Mottled glaze to interior. Red earthenware fabric. 180mm diameter base.
122. Mottled ware rim sherd. Upper surface of rim is shaped and concave. Red earthenware fabric. 300mm diameter.
123. Dark mottled ware rolled rim. Very fine with all-over glaze. Red earthenware fabric. 300mm diameter.

Slip-trailed wares

A total of 1067 slip-trailed sherds (11% of the total assemblage) were identified from the 2014-15 excavations, the majority of which used a predominantly red earthenware fabric, onto which a red slip wash had been applied. Decoration using a buff slip was then applied, and a clear lead glaze finally applied over both.

Small fine open-wares (cups/mugs or beakers).

Base sherds recovered from the 2014-15 excavations provided the most useful information with regards size and form of the smaller, finer slip-trailed vessels. In many cases the rim sherds, which were plentiful, were so fine that they had become too fragmented to provide an accurate vessel diameter. However, what was apparent from the sherds was that the rims of these vessels were slightly out-turned or everted.

Around 581 (54%) of the slip-trailed sherds were presumed to have come from small, fine drinking vessels, including flared cups and straight-sided mugs or beakers. Rims measured between 60mm and 150mm in diameter and various forms were identified, some of which, as identified by Rutter in the 1970's, comprised small, fine tea cups (nos. 124-5).

The 2014-15 excavations identified two near complete vessels with single, looped handles, which appeared to be a form of large cup, one with a flared body (no. 132) and the other in the style of a necked cup (no. 133). Both were around 150mm in diameter at the rim and 100mm tall, with a footring around the base. These were possibly too large to have been used as drinking vessels and could have been a form of the Buckley 'dip pot' for transferring milk from one vessel to another. An assortment of sherds potentially originating from straight-sided mugs or beakers were also noted among the slip-trailed wares (no. 126-131).

Decorative patterns within the slip-trailed wares varied considerably, the two near complete pots described above employing horizontal stripes or zig-zags around the circumference of the pot. In many cases, dots, dashes or zig-zags were applied around the rims.

Flared, shallow bowls

Around 27 everted rim sherds were identified with slip-trailed decoration, measuring around 150mm and 220mm in diameter (nos. 134-142 and 144-146). Given their form and decoration, the smaller vessels are assumed to have been utilised as table ware, while some of the slightly larger vessels may have been utilised in the kitchen or pantry.

Slightly flared, single-handled vessels

Following a style already seen within the blackware and mottled ware glazes, the full profile of a single-handled, slightly flared vessel with a rolled rim was identified (no. 149). Slip-trailed decoration had been applied to the rim and outside of the vessel. This measured 200mm in diameter at the rim, 160mm at the base and 112mm high. Additional rim and base sherds, which appear to have originated from similar vessels were also seen with slip-trailed decoration (nos. 143 and 148).

Large, flared bowls

Around 14% of the slip-trailed ware is represented by a type of large, flared bowl with a rolled or everted rim. The bowls measured around 100mm high (see Figure 32) with rim diameters between 260mm and 350mm. One near complete bowl in this style was recovered during the 2014 archaeological evaluation at Withen Cottage, carried out in the field adjacent to Elfed School, (no. 156). This style of vessel was also being produced in a brown glaze and is likely to have been utilised in the kitchen or pantry.

Miscellaneous

A fine, in-turned rim sherd (see no. 147) with spotted white slip decoration was recovered from the 2014-15 excavations. This appeared to form part of a straight-sided vessel, possibly a jar and is likely to have originally had a lid.

Catalogue of slip-trailed wares

124. Slip-trailed base sherd, probably from a fine cup, found in 1974. Rounded footring. Vessel body flares outwards from base. Red earthenware fabric. 75mm diameter base.
125. Fine, slip-trailed base sherd with angular footring. Vessel body flares outwards from base. Delicate handle stub visible. All over glaze with buff slip trailed decoration to exterior. Red earthenware fabric. 60mm diameter base.
126. Fine slip-trailed rim sherd found in 1974. Rim is slightly out-turned. Dark buff/brown fabric. 100mm diameter.
127. Slip-trailed, plain base sherd, probably from a tankard/mug or straight sided cup. Straight-sided vessel. Buff slip decoration to interior. No visible glaze on exterior. Red earthenware fabric. 100mm diameter.
128. Slip-trailed, everted rim sherd. All over glaze. Red earthenware fabric. 130mm diameter.
129. Slip-trailed out-turned rim sherd. Vessel body flares subtly outwards below rim. Dotted buff slip decoration around top of rim. Red earthenware fabric. 120mm diameter.
130. Slip-trailed base sherd from a possible mug found in 1974. Red earthenware fabric. 98mm diameter base.
131. Slip-trailed base sherd, probably from a large cup. Plain rounded base and straight sided vessel. All over glaze, terminating 23mm above base on exterior with red under-slip. Buff slip-trailed decoration to exterior. Red earthenware fabric. 120mm diameter base.
132. Slip-trailed (almost complete) flared cup with single handle. All over glaze, terminating 25mm above base on exterior, with red under-slip. Buff slip-trailed decoration to exterior comprising a double horizontal zig-zag below rim and double horizontal lines below this. Decorative footring. Red earthenware fabric. 140mm diameter.

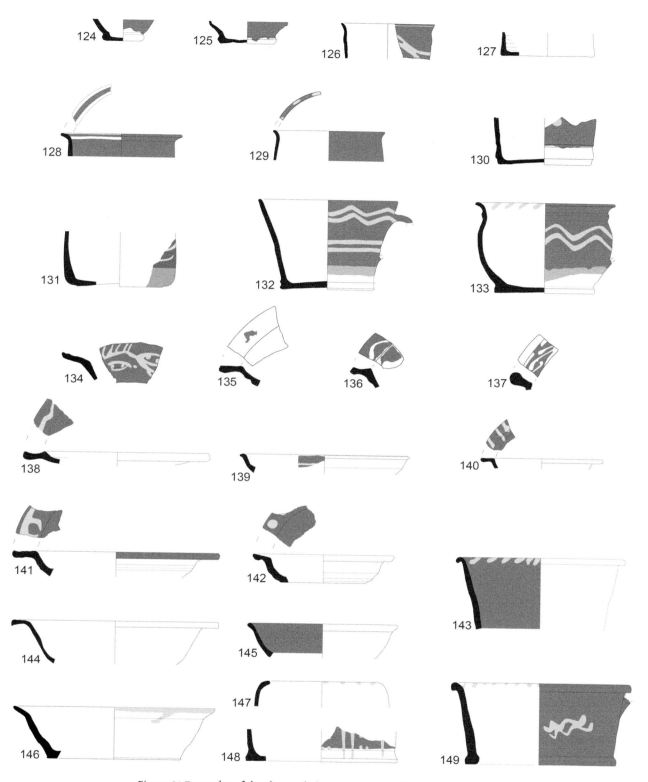

Figure 31 Examples of the slip-trailed wares from Price's Pottery. Scale 1:4.

133. Slip-trailed (almost complete) necked cup with single handle. All over glaze, terminating around 27mm above base on exterior with red under-slip. Buff slip-trailed decoration to exterior comprising horizontal, double zig zag and spotted decoration around interior of rim. Out-turned rim and straight-sided footring. Red earthenware fabric. 147mm diameter.

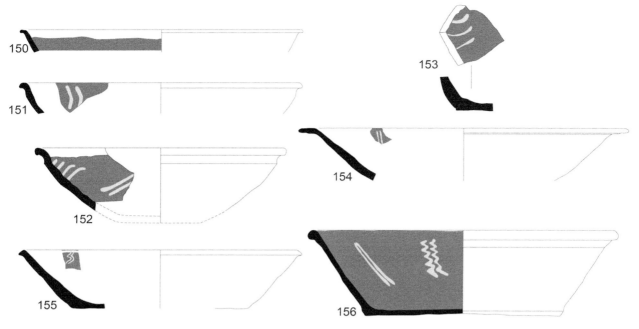

Figure 32 Examples of the larger slip-trailed wares from Price's Pottery. Scale 1:4.

134. Wide everted rim sherd found in 1974, Rutter Type 60. Comprehensive trailed decoration around the rim. Probable flared bowl.

135. Slip-trailed bowl/plate with a wide, everted rim. Yellow glaze and dark brown slip detail. 17th century. Red earthenware fabric. 280mm diameter.

136. Slip-trailed probable bowl with an everted rim. Dark brown glaze with buff slip decoration. Red slipwash to underside. Red earthenware fabric. 200mm diameter.

137. Slip-trailed thickened rim sherd with dark brown glaze and buff slip decoration. Parallels seen at pinfold Lane. Red earthenware fabric. Dated 1680-1720. 350mm diameter.

138. Slip-trailed rim sherd, probably from a shallow bowl measuring 200mm in diameter. Slip-trailed with buff slip. Rim is everted and concave. No visible exterior glaze.

139. Fine slip-trailed rim sherd, probably from a shallow bowl. Glaze to interior with buff slip-trailed decoration. No external glaze. Red earthenware fabric. 180mm diameter.

140. Slip-trailed probable bowl with a flat, everted rim. Slip-trailed with buff slip. Red earthenware fabric. 130mm rim diameter.

141. Slip-trailed, flat, everted rim sherd. Glaze to interior and rim. Buff slip trailed decoration. Red earthenware fabric. 220mm diameter.

142. Fine slip-trailed bowl. Yellow slip-trailed decoration to interior and rim. No external glaze. Red earthenware fabric. 150mm diameter.

143. Slip-trailed possible straight-sided bowl with a hooked rim. All over glaze with buff slip-trailed decoration around interior of rim. Red earthenware fabric. 160mm rim diameter.

144. Slip-trailed everted rim sherd. Glaze to interior and rim with buff slip-trailed decoration. Red earthenware fabric. 220mm diameter.

145. Fine, slip-trailed rim sherd. Glazed interior, slip-washed exterior. Red earthenware fabric. 160mm diameter.

146. Shallow, slip-trailed bowl 55mm high found in 1974. Red earthenware fabric with slip-trailed decoration around the rim. 215mm diameter.

147. Fine slip-trailed in-turned rim sherd. Buff slip-trailed decoration. Red earthenware fabric. 90mm diameter.

148. Slip-trailed base sherd with slight squared footring. Straight-sided vessel. All-over glaze, terminating 16mm above the base on exterior. Brown glaze with buff slip-trailed decoration. Red earthenware fabric. 160mm diameter base.

149. Slip-trailed vessel with handle stub. All-over brown glaze with buff slip trailed decoration to rim and exterior. Red earthenware fabric with small percentage of buff clay. 200mm diameter.
150. Slip-trailed probable large bowl with an everted rim. Glaze to interior only, terminating 8mm below rim. No external glaze. Red earthenware fabric. 300mm diameter.
151. Slip-trailed probable basin. Slightly out-turned rim with indent below to exterior. Buff slip trailed decoration on red under-slip with lead glaze above terminating just below the rim. Red earthenware fabric. 300mm diameter.
152. Slip-trailed probable flared bowl/dish found in 1974. Red earthenware fabric with slip-trailed decoration to interior. Slightly out-turned rim with indented underside. 370mm diameter.
153. Fragment of a slab made dish or meat platter found in 1974.
154. Slip-trained probable basin with a flat, everted rim. Slip-trailed decoration to interior in buff slip, terminating just below the inner rim. Red earthenware fabric. 350mm diameter.
155. Slip-trailed flared bowl or small basin with an everted rim. Red earthenware fabric with slip-trailed decoration to the interior. No visible glaze to exterior. 350mm diameter.
156. Near complete slip trailed bowl or basin. Glaze to internal with buff slip decoration in alternating pairs of lines and zig zags. Red earthenware fabric. Diameter 330mm.

Brown ware

A 'brown ware' was most almost certainly being produced at Price's Pottery, often under-coated with a red slip. Lead-glazed sherds were also common, whereby a red earthenware vessel was given a clear glaze. Brown ware sherds and lead-glazed sherds are discussed together here. Sherds classified as brown ware accounted for 290 (3%) of the total sherd count, with a similar quantity of 283 (2%) being classified as lead-glazed.

It should also be noted that it is likely that some of the sherds catalogued as brown ware were originally part of slip-trailed vessels, particularly large flared bowls, and represent areas of the vessel where the slip-trailed decoration had not been applied. For the purpose of the catalogue, any sherd with no obvious slip-trailed decoration was recorded as brown ware or lead-glazed.

Small, fine, open wares

The largest proportion of the brown wares (52%) consisted of smaller fine-wares, probably drinking vessels. Base sherds with a rounded footring and flared body were common, probably from cups of varying size (see nos. 158, 161, 162 and 166–169). Straighter-sided vessels were also being produced, probably tankards (nos. 163-164) and beakers or mugs (nos. 159, 160 and 165).

Straight-sided, single handled bowl

Rutter identified a straight-sided vessel with evidence of a single handle and a slight rounded footring (see no. 171). This style of vessel is similar to other examples seen within the blackware, mottled ware and slip-trailed wares, with the handle extending outwards from just above the base.

Small flared bowls

Rutter also identified the full profile of a small brown glazed flared bowl (no. 170), measuring 145mm in diameter and 45mm high and at least four other similar examples (no. 174) were found in the more recent excavations of 2014-15, as well as some slightly larger examples (no. 175).

Globular vessels

Two brown-glazed sherds from vessels with rounded bodies were identified by Rutter. One was a flat, everted rim sherd (no. 176), measuring 195mm in diameter, below which the body of the vessel flared outwards to form a rounded profile. Lines of reeding were visible on the body of the pot. Similar vessels have been noted at Prescott's Pottery and dated to 1740-1803 (Rutter 1977). The other was a base sherd (no. 172) displaying a pronounced, angled footring of 138mm diameter. Both sherds were considered likely to have come from either a rounded jar or chamber pot.

Catalogue of brown wares

157. Rim found in 1974, possibly of a straight sided kitchen jar. Red earthenware fabric. 52mm diameter.
158. Base sherd, probably from a cup, with a deep footring and flaring sides, found in 1974. 50mm diameter
159. Lead-glazed upright rim sherd, slightly out-turned. All over glaze. Straight-sided vessel profile. Red earthenware fabric. 100mm diameter.
160. Lead-glazed probable straight-sided cup or mug handle. Red earthenware fabric.
161. Dark brown glazed base sherd, probably a cup, with narrow, squared footring. Body of vessel flares outwards from base. Red under-slip beneath glaze. Glaze to interior, nothing visible on exterior. Red earthenware fabric. 90mm diameter base.
162. Dark brown glazed base sherd, probably a cup, with narrow, rounded footring. Body of vessel flares outwards from base. All over glaze, terminating just above the footring on the exterior. Red earthenware fabric. 80mm diameter base.
163. Brown glazed base sherd, probably a mug, with footring, found in 1974. Remnants of a handle are visible on one side. Red earthenware fabric. 82mm diameter base.
164. Brown glazed, base sherd, probably a cup or mug with angled footring. Straight-sided vessel. All over glaze, dribbled to just above base on exterior. Red earthenware fabric. 100mm diameter base.
165. Dark brown glazed base sherd from a large tankard, mug or jug with thick, angular footring. Vessel body flares outwards sharply from base. Glazed on interior, with red slip wash visible on exterior. 100mm diameter base.
166. Dark brown glazed (overfired) base sherd with slight footring. Body of vessel flares outwards from base. All over glaze, terminating just above footring on exterior. Red earthenware fabric. 90mm diameter base.
167. Dark brown glazed base sherd, probably a cup, with angular footring. Body of vessel flares outwards from base. All over glaze, terminating just above the base on exterior. Red earthenware fabric. 100mm diameter base.
168. Lead-glazed, plain base sherd. Vessel flares outwards from base, before straightening 15mm above base. All over glaze, terminating 15mm above base on exterior with red under-slip. Red earthenware fabric. 100mm diameter base.
169. Brown glazed base sherd found in 1974. Angled footring at base. All-over glaze terminating just above the footring on exterior. Remnants of a handle visible on body of vessel. 110mm diameter base.
170. Brown glazed dish with complete profile found in 1974. The rim and interior are glazed. Red earthenware fabric. 145mm diameter.
171. Brown glazed base sherd found in 1974. Slight rounded footring and handle stub visible just above the footring. Red earthenware fabric. 175mm diameter base.
172. Mid brown glazed base sherd from a possible flared jar or chamber pot found in 1974. Deep angled footring with all-over glaze down onto footring. 138mm diameter base r.
173. Dark brown glazed, plain base sherd. Glaze to interior only. Red earthenware fabric. 110mm diameter base.
174. Dark brown glazed probable jar or chamber pot with out-turned rim with found in 1974. The body of the pot flares outwards beneath the rim with visible lines of decorative reeding. 185mm diameter.
175. Brown glazed, plain base sherd. Brown glaze to interior. No visible glaze to exterior. Red earthenware fabric. 110mm diameter base.
176. Dark brown glazed, flat everted rim sherd found in 1974. The body of the vessel flares outwards below the rim in the style of a chamber pot and has bands of reeding below the rim. Red earthenware fabric. 195mm diameter. Similar vessel have been noted at Prescot's Pottery (Site 7) and dated to 1740-1803.

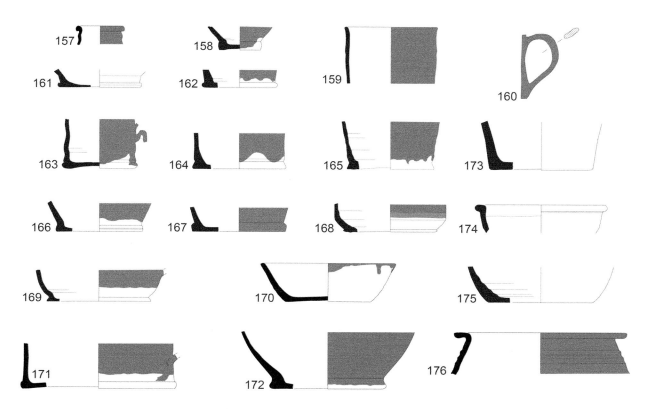

Figure 33 Examples of the smaller brown ware vessels from Price's Pottery. Scale 1:4.

Large vessels (kitchen/pantry/dairy wares)

A number of larger vessels were also being produced with a brown glaze, as evidenced by a series of rim sherds between 220mm and 350mm in diameter. Some of these included fine ware vessels with a rolled rim, possibly from large storage jars (see no. 177) or flared bowls (see nos. 178 and 180).

Larger flared bowls with simple, slightly out-turned rims of around 300mm diameter were produced in brown ware (see nos. 181, 183 and 184) and some thicker bodied flared bowls (see no. 186) with a wide, everted rim.

Upright jars with various rim styles were also being produced, similar forms being traditionally referred to in Buckley as varieties of the pancheon. These thicker bodied vessels included examples of collared and ribbed rims (see no. 179) thickened everted rims (see no. 185), hammerhead rims (see no. 187) and up-turned squared rims (see no. 182), the latter of which is likely to have accommodated a lid.

Miscellaneous

The neck of a small kitchen jar (see no. 157) was also identified by Rutter, and in the recent excavations, a plain, thick base sherd (see no. 173), which appears to have come from an upright vessel, possibly a jar or jug.

177. Fine, dark brown glazed, rolled rim sherd. Vessel flares out below the rim. All over glaze. Red earthenware fabric. 250mm diameter.
178. Lead-glazed bevelled and indented rim sherd. Glaze to interior. Red earthenware fabric. 240mm diameter.
179. Dark-brown glazed vessel with glaze to interior and exterior. Partially glazed collared and ribbed rim. Red earthenware fabric. 280mm diameter.
180. Dark brown glazed rim. All-over glaze. Red earthenware fabric. 200mm diameter.

181. Brown-glazed, thickened and out-turned rim sherd. Glaze to interior and upper rim. Red slip-wash to exterior. Red earthenware fabric. 300mm diameter.
182. Dark brown glazed rim sherd. Dark brown glaze to interior and rim with red under-slip. No external glaze visible. Red earthenware fabric. 350mm diameter.
183. Dark brown glazed probable basin with slightly thickened rim. Dark brown glaze to interior, with red under-slip terminating just below the rim. Similar forms measuring 280-300mm diameter. Red earthenware fabric. 320mm diameter.
184. Brown-glazed pancheon with glaze to interior and rim. Red slip wash to exterior. Everted and up-turned rim, 30mm wide. Red earthenware fabric. 300mm diameter.

Figure 34 Examples of the larger brown ware vessels from Price's Pottery. Scale 1:4.

185. Dark-brown glazed upright vessel with dark brown glaze to interior – terminating 45mm below the rim. No external glaze visible. Thick, everted rim measuring 24mm wide. Red earthenware fabric. 320mm diameter.
186. Dark-brown glazed pancheon with glaze to interior and rim. Red slip wash to exterior. Wide everted rim measuring 40mm wide. Red earthenware fabric. 350mm diameter.
187. Dark-brown glazed vessel with glaze to interior and rim. Red slip wash to exterior. Hammerhead rim measuring 30mm wide. Red earthenware fabric. 350mm diameter.
188. Dark-brown glazed plain base, 14mm thick. Red earthenware fabric. 320mm diameter base.

Press-moulded slipware

The press-moulded slipware represents 5% of the sherds recovered during the 2014-15 excavations, having been recovered from both the Elfed School playing field and the archaeological evaluation trench in the adjacent field at Withen Cottage in 2014. The majority of the press-moulded sherds are from platters or dishes and are reminiscent of vessels found at Pinfold Lane. Most of the Price's sherds are of early to mid-18th century date, with a few later sherds also appearing.

A wide range of decorative techniques were used, predominantly slip-trailing but also combing, joggling, feathering and marbling. The use of two coloured slips (see nos. 190-192 and 195) tended to be most common in Buckley between about 1720 and 1760. Also distinctive of this time was the use of a type of mould which pressed two indented lines around the inside of the base of the vessels (see nos. 194-5).

Many of the press-moulded sherds from Price's were rim sherds displaying pie crust detail around the edge of the rim, a technique which was first introduced in the 17th century in Buckley, using cockle shells. Pinching was later used, particularly in the first half of the 18th century, but later press-moulded wares from Buckley eventually became much cruder and decorative details like those mentioned above were eventually abandoned for simple straight cut rims and simplified slip decoration to allow vessels to be produced quickly and cheaply. A press-moulded rim sherd from a meat dish (no. *193*), thought to date to around 1840-50, shows just how much simpler the rims and slip decoration had become by this time.

Catalogue of press-moulded wares

189. Press-moulded rim sherd. Rim is bevelled with pie-crust detail and an indented ridge 18mm from rim edge. Overall yellow slip with dark brown slip trailed detail and a lead glaze. Red earthenware fabric. 220mm diameter.
190. Press-moulded shallow dish dated 1720-60. Rim is rounded and slightly down-turned with pie-crust detail. Three slips used, with dark brown as a base and buff and orange trailed decoration. Red earthenware fabric. 350mm diameter.
191. Press-moulded probable dish with a flat, everted rim and pie-crust detail. Yellow slip overall with dark brown joggled slip. Red earthenware fabric. 220mm diameter.
192. Press-moulded dish dated 1720-60. Rim is wide, flat everted with pie-crust detail. Three slips used, with dark brown overall and buff and orange trailed decoration. Red earthenware fabric. 350mm diameter.
193. Press-moulded rim sherd from meat dish dated 1840-50. Dark brown glaze overall with buff slip trailed decoration. Red earthenware fabric.
194. Fine, press-moulded sherd dated to 1750-1780, with yellow slip overall and dark brown slip decoration. Sherd has two ridges visible which would have run around internal base of the vessel. Red earthenware fabric.
195. Press-moulded sherd dated to 1750-1780, with dark brown slip overall and buff slip decoration. Sherd has two ridges visible which would have run around internal base of the vessel. Red earthenware fabric.

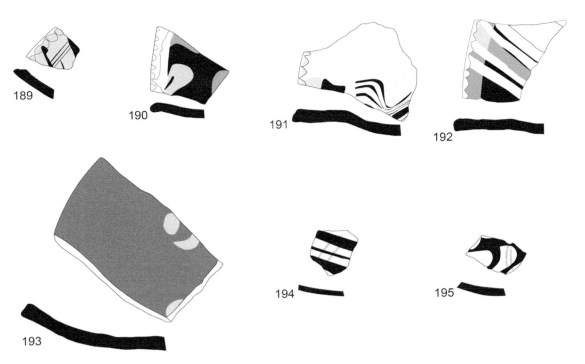

Figure 35 Examples of the pressed wares from Price's Pottery. Scale 1:4.

Agate-bodied ware

A very small quantity (8 sherds) of agate-bodied ware was identified within the Price's pottery assemblage. The body of these vessels is composed of mixed clays, designed to create different colours on the surface of the vessel on firing. It is not especially common in Buckley, although agate-bodied wares have been found on the site of Prescott's Pottery (Site 7).

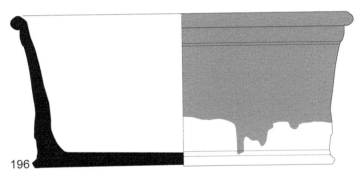

Figure 36 Example of an agate bodied-bowl found at Price's Pottery. Scale 1:4.

A small body sherd found at Price's is perhaps the best example of the effect of the mixing of the two clay. The sherd was not glazed.

Also found during the 2014-15 excavations was a near complete agate-bodied bowl (no. 196), measuring 240mm in diameter and 100mm tall. This vessel was similar in form to some of the slightly flared, single handled bowls identified within the blackware, mottled ware and slip-trailed assemblages.

Such a small quantity of agate-bodied ware suggests it was not in such high demand as the other wares that were regularly being produced at Price's Pottery and while some sherds may have originated from elsewhere, the unglazed sherd could suggest that agate bodied wares were being experimented with at Price's Pottery, or perhaps produced occasionally on demand.

Miscellaneous

Sgraffito

One sherd of pottery with a red slip wash to the external face and a thick buff, matte glaze to the interior had signs of sgraffito decoration. This type of ware was usually of a red fabric with a white slip coating, through which a decoration would have been scratched to expose the red clay beneath. The vessel would then have been glazed. As yet, sgraffito is only known to have been produced elsewhere in Buckley, at Brookhill (Site 1), and given that this sherd appears to be isolated, it seems unlikely that it was produced at Price's.

Cooking pot

Two fragments of 17th-century cooking pot were identified, having been thrown using fireclay. This clay was usually taken straight from the ground and was not allowed to weather as other clays were. Fire clay was typically used for vessels that needed to withstand extremely high temperatures – such as saggars, cooking pots or crucibles. Given the small quantity of cooking pot sherds identified within the sample from Price's, it is doubtful that they were producing vessels of this type there.

Yellow ware

One body sherd and one rim sherd measuring 400mm in diameter were recorded, which are thought to date to the late 19th century. These appear to have been part of a large flared bowl or basin and is unlikely to have ever been in production at the site.

Unglazed wares

Around 10% of the pottery recovered during the excavations was unglazed, most of which appeared to be fragments from relatively plain, straight sided vessels with rolled rims between 140 and 220mm in diameter. Some of the bases present undoubtedly represent the remains of plant pots, but it was also apparent within the assemblage that there were some 'unglazed' fragments from finer vessels with a rolled rim, as well as some smaller vessels, probably cups and jugs. It is likely that some of the unglazed sherds simply represent the 'unglazed' areas of otherwise glazed vessels, with some examples clearly having originated from larger vessels, such as pancheons, in which the rims were often left unglazed.

Handles

Of the total number of pottery sherds recovered during the 2014-15 excavations, 550 were handle fragments, the majority (419 sherds) assumed to have come from cups. Most were rod handles with an oval cross section and attached at both ends to the side of the vessels to form a loop. A small quantity of side handles, and strap handles particularly from larger vessels were also identified.

Kiln furniture

Saggars

Smaller, delicate pots would have been placed inside large, coarseware vessels known as saggars to protect them from the heat of the kiln. Large quantities of broken saggar were recovered during the excavations, which would be expected in the context of a dump of waste material. The saggars from Price's appear to have been circular with straight sides and made from buff or red fire clay, with red fire clay appearing to have been preferred. Examples with full profiles ranged between 132mm and 152mm high and between 318mm and 564mm in diameter. The base was always plain, and the rims thickened into varying profiles. Some examples displayed ventilation holes and two fragments of a saggar lid were also recorded.

Separators

A total of 250 separators were found during the 2014-15 excavations. These small pieces of clay were often placed around the rims of vessels to prevent them sticking to the pots they were stacked with during firing. The majority of the separators from Price's Pottery were relatively small, further highlighting the predominance of the smaller, finer vessels that appear to have been more regularly produced there.

However, some larger spacers were also found and appear to have been used to separate larger, wide rimmed vessels. The separators were always of red clay, and the larger ones often bare the finger prints of the potter where the clay had been squeezed onto the rim. Separators would have been knocked off after firing, sometimes leaving an indentation of the pot rim in the clay and evidence on the rim itself of where the separator had been attached.

Stilts

A small number of stilts (13) were recovered, which were small, cone shaped and of red earthenware. Pots were sometimes placed onto stilts for support during firing and to prevent glazed pieces from sticking to each other.

Building materials

Although the excavations revealed no *in situ* remains for the kiln or pottery buildings, a large quantity of brick debris was present across the site, of which only a small sample was retained. This included two fragments of red, hand-made brick, manufactured from a gritty clay with frequent white grit inclusions of around 5mm in size. It is possible these were fragments of the kiln base and measured 114mm (4½ inches) wide by 70mm (2¾ inches) thick. As they were incomplete, it was not possible to obtain length measurements for any of the bricks recovered during the excavations, although it was noted that at least one of the bricks appeared to be tapered – measuring 130mm (7 inches) at its widest end and 110mm (4 inches) at the narrower end, where it had broken. It is possible this was used in the construction of part of the kiln.

Conclusions

Although there is no documentary evidence that the pottery was operational before 1783, the results of the 1974 and 2014-15 excavations suggest that pottery was being manufactured at Price's Pottery as early as the first half of the 18th century, perhaps 60 years earlier than had been previously appreciated. The pottery continued in production until around 1868 and during the whole of its operational life, appears to have remained in the Price family, passed down from one generation to the next.

Unfortunately, the excavations produced no evidence for the pottery buildings or kiln owing to the extent of modern landscaping across the site, although a large quantity of associated material was encountered, including brick rubble, part of a kiln shelf, saggars, stilts and separators, not to mention the large quantities of pottery wasters. Firing waste such as clinker and ash was also identified. If any of the original pottery buildings do survive it may be possible remains of these lie to the north of the school playing fields in the gardens of nearby houses.

The effect of the later interventions across the site of Price's Pottery, particularly the construction of housing and the landscaping for the school playing fields in the 1970s is reflected in the quality of the pottery recovered from the site. When compared to some of the other Buckley pottery excavations where vessels recovered have been much more complete, at Price's the sherds were very fragmented and very small, which often made identification difficult. The most complete examples were recovered from the fill of a deep pit that had been backfilled with pottery wasters, the depth of which had luckily exceeded the interventions necessary for the construction of the school playing fields and thus leaving these vessels more intact.

As Rutter (1977) noted, the majority of the pottery recovered from this particular area of the pottery could in theory be derived from one failed kiln firing and cannot necessarily be taken as representative of the full range of wares that were in production throughout the life time of Price's Pottery. However, on the basis of the pottery recovered to date, the following conclusions can be drawn.

In comparison to some of the other Buckley potteries, Price's was a relatively small site, producing predominantly smaller, fine wares, rather than the larger vessels or industrial wares for which Buckley is well known. It appears that fine, hollow-ware vessels up to 140mm in diameter were regularly being produced at Price's. These were made in a variety of glazes, including blackware, slip-trailed, mottled ware, brown ware and lead-glazed. A large quantity of these (around 23% of the overall assemblage) are assumed to have been fine ware cups, mugs and tankards, and although there were variations of each type, the overall styles were being produced consistently within each glaze type.

Fine ware bowls also appear to have been produced regularly as well as a range of larger fine wares, particularly globular vessels with a rolled or everted rim and a single handle, very much like a chamber pot in appearance. This style of vessel appears consistently, particularly in the blackware, mottled ware and brown ware. Similarly, a style of bowl with slightly flared sides and a single handle was seen in all of the above wares, as well as some slip-trailed examples, though the purpose of this type of vessel is uncertain.

In addition to the finer wares, Price's also seems to have been producing quantities of slightly coarser kitchen or pantry ware, which although not strictly coarseware, were certainly more robust than the finewares. These wares included jugs, upright jars and large flared bowls, the latter appearing to be a slightly smaller form of the traditional Buckley basin, being commonly fired with a slip-trailed decoration or a brown glaze.

Apart from the saggars and the few sherds of cooking pot, the largest vessels recovered from Price's Pottery included an assortment of large flared bowls with wide everted rims (more often referred to as variations of the Buckley 'pan-mug' or 'pancheon'), and large upright vessels, probably storage jars, with a thick, but narrow everted rim. These were most predominant in the blackware and brown ware.

Overall, the excavations across the site of Price's Pottery have gathered useful information regarding the range of products that were being produced there and its period of operation. A 'house style' certainly seems to have been adopted, with distinct forms that were being repeatedly made in varying glazes. The press-moulded wares particularly suggest this was perhaps one of the earlier wares being produced at Prices in the early 18th century, perhaps taking advantage of the market forces of the time and black iridescent glazes featuring more towards the end of the pottery's lifetime.

A Gazetteer of Buckley Potteries

In the following gazetteer each site is referenced firstly in accordance with a numbering sequence developed by Peter Davey for sites 1 to 19 (Davey 1976a), and also with reference to a Primary Record Number (PRN), recorded in the regional Historic Environment Record (PRN), maintained by CPAT.

Buckley Potteries Site 1, Brookhill Pottery

PRN 101670
SJ 2794 6554
Date: 1640-1720

The earliest post-medieval site in Buckley, Brookhill has been dated by the clay tobacco pipes found throughout the excavation (see below) to around 1640 to 1720. The site occupies an overgrown plot within which the ruins of a 19th-century house and stable can be identified.

It was excavated by James Bentley between 1974 and 1985 (see Figure 37), revealing up to 15 kiln bases, ten of which were defined by shallow depressions filled with ash, coal dust, kiln furniture and wasters. These appear to have been clamp kilns with infilled material providing a firm refractory floor which, being porous, also acted as an underfloor flue. Two smaller kilns were set directly on the ground (Amery and Davey 1979, 51). The kilns all had internal diameters of between 1.5m and 2m (Gruffydd 2010, 88).

Small-scale excavations were undertaken by CPAT in September 2016 (Hankinson 2017), to the west of the area of known kilns excavated previously by Bentley, although partly reinvestigating other, later features revealed by the earlier excavations.

The earliest wares include complex slip-decorated thrown bowls, executed in both *sgraffito* and trailing techniques (Figure 3, b and c), porringers with press-moulded handles, a female figurine and large tripod cooking vessels. Later wares include mottled ware tankards and bowls, slipware dishes and black- and brown-glazed cups and storage vessels (Davey 1976a, 18).

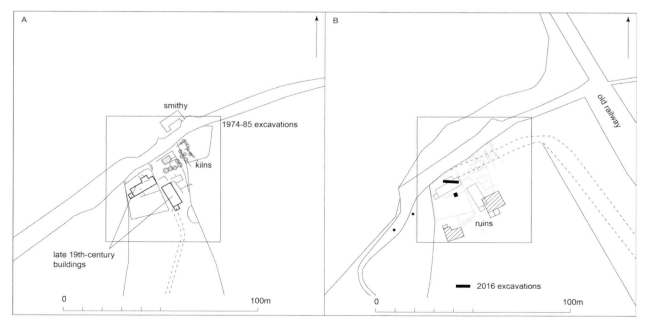

Figure 37 Site 1, Brookhill Pottery. A – excavated evidence and 19th-century buildings, B – present day showing the location of pottery features in grey.

Events

Excavation 1974-85 (PRN 129925; see references below)
Excavation 2016 (PRN 140153; Hankinson 2017)

Status

Unscheduled

Condition

Partly excavated. The remainder of the site lies within a pasture field.

Potential

Although the site has seen substantial excavations its full extent is unknown and there is likely to be significant potential for further buried remains to the east of the excavated area. To the west of the area containing the kilns, evidence of features potentially relating to the pottery appears to remain *in situ*.

Associated records

None

References

Amery 1979
Amery and Davey 1979
Bentley & Harrison 1975a
Bentley & Harrison 1975b
Bentley 1976a
Bentley 1976b
Bentley 1977a
Bentley 1977b
Bentley 1978a
Bentley 1978b
Bentley 1979a
Bentley 1979b
Bentley 1984a
Bentley 1984b
Bentley 1984c
Bentley 1985a
Bentley 1985b
Bentley 1985c
Bentley n.d.
Davey 1976a, 18
Davey and Longworth 2001, 62-72
Gruffydd 2010, 88
Hankinson 2017
Higgins 1983
Longworth 1999
Longworth 2004
Longworth 2005
Longworth and McLaughlin Cook 2000
Messham 1956, 31-61

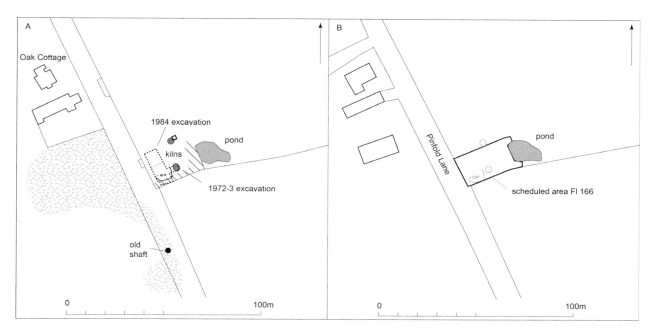

Figure 38 Site 2, Cottrell's Pottery. A – detail from the Ordnance Survey mapping of 1874, showing excavated areas; B – present day and the extent of the scheduled area.

Buckley Potteries Site 2, Cottrell's Pottery

PRN 101671
SJ 2752 6553
Date: late 17th century to early 19th century

The pottery lies on the east side of Pinfold Lane and was originally discovered when a dump of wasters was found, having been eroded at the edge of a pond. Partial excavation in 1972-3 produced a series of well-stratified wares including kiln furniture belonging to the 17th and 18th centuries (Bentley and Harrison 1973). Further excavations were conducted in 1984, revealing two beehive kilns of the updraught type with eight flues, together with a small circular pit thought to be for grinding galena to make the glaze and two stone-lined pits, one for blunging and the other for the preparation of white slip for decorating the pots. The excavations also found evidence for later activity on the site, post-dating the pottery, comprising the foundations of an 18th-century building and a stone wall and brick floor belonging to a 19th-century building (McNeil 1984).

The pottery appears to have been in operation from the late 17th century until the early 19th century, and is depicted on estate maps of 1757 and 1781, the latter identifying the tenant as Benjamin Cottrell with the plot being occupied by a mug-kiln and house. Between at least 1804 and 1815 the pottery was operated by William Leach.

While the kiln furniture and clay tobacco pipes are similar in form and fabric to those from the contemporary pottery at Brookhill (Site 1), the pottery is noticeably different. Bowls with simple slip-trailing round the rim are restricted to Pinfold Lane and there is a wider range of press-moulded dishes (Figure 3 d-f). Both Pinfold Lane and Brookhill produced mottled ware tankards and bowls, but Pinfold Lane has a wider range of bodies and slip decoration. Both sites produced a large collection of black-glazed wares (Davey 1976a, 18; Davey and Longworth 2001, 62-72). The site is now farmland.

Events

Excavation 1972-3 (PRN 58092)
Excavation 1984 (PRN 70816; McNeil 1985)

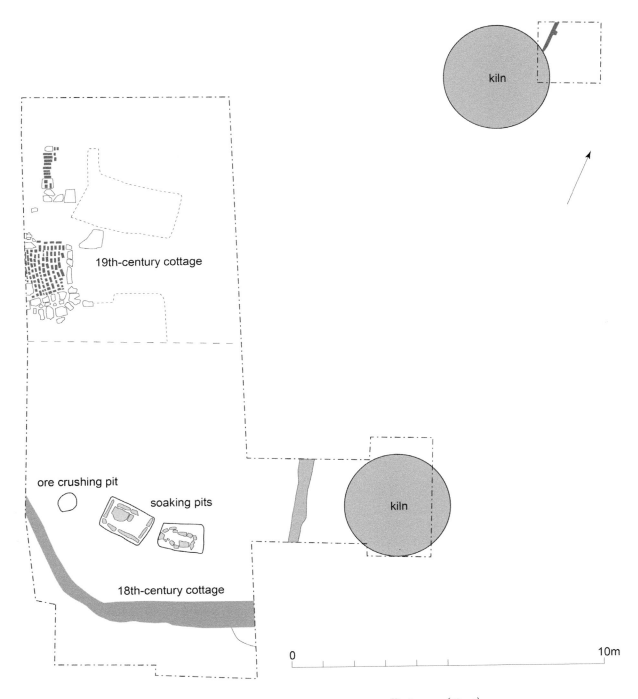

Figure 39 Plan of the 1984 excavations at Cottrell's Pottery (Site 2).

Status

Scheduled (Fl 166)

Condition

Partly excavated, demonstrating good sub-surface preservation

Potential

The unexcavated areas are likely to contain significant remains and there is some uncertainty regarding the extent of the pottery and the exact location of the excavated features.

Associated records

None

References

Bentley 1979a
Bentley and Harrison 1973a
Bentley and Harrison 1973b
Bentley and Harrison 1974a
Davey 1975b
Davey 1976a, 18
Davey 1987
Davey and Longworth 2001, 62-72
Davey et al. 2014
Davey et al. 2014
Knight 2001
McNeil 1984
McNeil 1985a
McNeil 1985b
Speakman n.d./a
Speakman n.d./b

Buckley Potteries Site 3, Taylor's Pottery

PRN 101673
SJ 2689 6533
Date: 18th-early 20th century

The site occupies an encroachment onto the common and a kiln is recorded here on the Ewloe Lordship map of 1757, which shows a single kiln on the common and a rectangular building within an enclosure. The *c.* 1780 Ewloe Estate map (no XII) lists the tenant as Joseph Codrell's sister, describing the land as

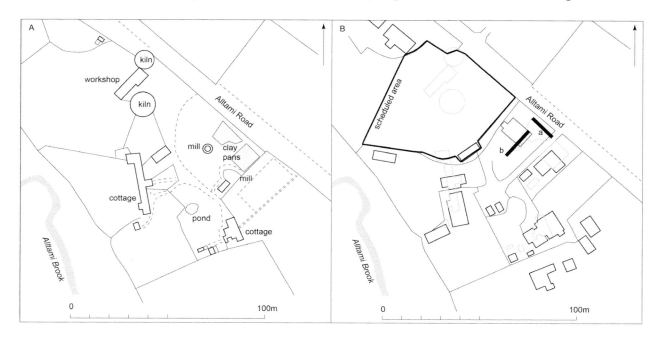

Figure 40 Site 3, Taylor's Pottery. A – detail from the Ordnance Survey mapping of 1874; B – present day showing the location of pottery features in grey and the location of the 2005 excavations.

occupied by crofts, house, mug-kiln and garden. Later records indicate that the pottery was operated by the Taylor family (John Taylor in 1815; Taylor and Son in 1860; and Charles Taylor in 1886). Some 19th-century pottery and kiln furniture has been recovered from gardens (Davey 1976a, 20).

The pottery complex straddled both sides of Alltami Road and the 1874 mapping shows two kilns, a mill (a blunger or pan mill) and numerous potters' workshops and houses. To the north-east of the road, located on the common, the map depicts two ponds, likely to be clay pans, linked by a watercourse, as well as a kiln which had been recorded in 1860 as a brick kiln. Later editions of the Ordnance Survey mapping, in 1899 and 1912, show that the pottery was still active with minor changes to the layout.

The site of two kilns, chimneys, drying sheds and blunging pits lie in rough pasture, an area which is now a scheduled monument (FL 165). A range of other structures and features to the south-east are partly beneath later buildings, although some structures, including workers' housing, may be incorporated into the extant buildings. The slight earthworks of clay pans, or settling tanks, can still be discerned among the vegetation on the north-east side of the road.

An evaluation in 2005 revealed the remains of a relatively well-preserved circular, brick-built structure, which is likely to be a blunger, or perhaps a pan mill, for processing clay. A large feature nearby is likely to be a clay pan, a shallow pool where clay was stored and weathered. Both features are depicted by the Ordnance Survey in 1874. Pottery from the excavations included some kiln furniture as well as pancheons, bowls and black-glazed storage jars of likely mid-19th- to early 20th-century date (Earthworks 2005).

Events

Excavation 2005 (PRN 129926; Earthworks 2005)

Status

Scheduled (Fl 165)

Condition

The main pottery site is well-preserved in pasture and two workers cottages are still occupied, though altered, while other pottery-related structures and features are also likely to survive, either having been incorporated into later buildings, or as sub-surface remains. The site of the mill and clay pans is now occupied by a house.

Potential

There is considerable potential for significant buried remains, both within the scheduled area and beyond. The 1m-resolution LiDAR data indicates earthworks which relate to several of the pottery structures depicted on late 19th-century map sources, while features such as a kiln and the clay pans located on the common are likely to be undisturbed.

Associated records

PRN 98307 clay pit
PRN 126525 brick kiln
PRN 128079 settling tanks

References

Davey 1976a, 20
Davey and Longworth 2001
Earthworks 2005

1757 Lordship of Ewloe map
1780 (circa) Ewloe Estate (Map XII)
1874/1884 Ordnance Survey 1st edition 25" map
1889 Ordnance Survey 2nd edition 25" map
1912 Ordnance Survey 3rd edition 25" map

Buckley Potteries Site 4, John Lewis Junior's Pottery

PRN 101674
SJ 2708 6509
Date: 19th century

A new pottery was built by John Lewis Junior around 1805 and worked until his death in 1831. His widow Mary continued the pottery after his death, and after she died it was run by Thomas Lewis. In 1860 it was tenanted by Jane Lewis, Thomas's widow, and was worked by Thomas Jones, who had married into the family (Messham 1956, 42).

A building is depicted here on the 1841 tithe survey, though no kiln is shown, while the Ordnance Survey 1st edition map, published in 1884, shows a single kiln with a rectangular building to the west and a number of smaller structures elsewhere on the site. Also shown are a probable clay pan adjacent to a circular feature which may be a blunger. A waste dump is depicted on the common, at the southern end of which is a circular feature which could be a kiln. Further to the south-east and, also on the common, are a number of clay pits together with a circular feature which may be another blunger. The pottery had evidently closed by 1899 and the kiln and main building had been levelled.

The site of the kiln and main pottery building, including the possible blunger and clay pan, which was still visible during the 1970s, along with an associated conduit, lies in a pasture field. Two ruinous brick buildings within the field are likely to be pottery sheds or workshops. A worker's cottage (PRN 129918) survives to the south-east, adjacent to another house which was also contemporary with the pottery. On the common there are two obvious mounds, only one of which is depicted on 19th-century map sources, though both are probably waste dumps, a small amount of 19th-century pottery and kiln furniture

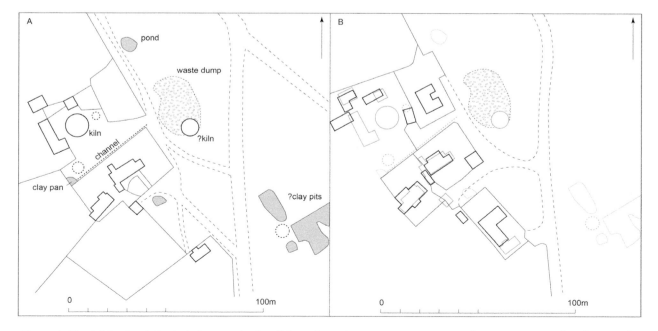

Figure 41 Site 4, John Lewis Junior's Pottery. A – detail from the Ordnance Survey mapping of 1884; B – present day showing the location of pottery features in grey.

having been recovered from there, as well as from the bungalow garden behind which the pottery is located (Davey 1976a, 20). There is, however, no sign of the circular feature depicted on later 19th-century mapping. The clay pits are still visible as earthworks in an area of scrub.

Events

None

Status

Unscheduled

Condition

Visible remains are restricted to those on the common, comprising the waste dump and clay pits. Some structures may survive, having been incorporated or reused as part of extant buildings, while the site of the kiln and pottery building are still undeveloped.

Potential

There is significant potential for the survival of buried remains to the rear of the modern bungalow, while the waste dump and possible kiln on the common appear undisturbed.

Associated records

PRN 129918

References

Davey 1976a, 20
Messham 1956, 42
1841 Tithe Survey
1884 Ordnance Survey 1st edition 25"

Buckley Potteries Site 5, Thomas Lewis' Pottery (also known as Willow Pottery)

PRN 101672
SJ 2746 6516
Date: 18th – mid 19th century

The older of the two potteries associated with the Lewis family appears on the Lordship of Ewloe map of 1757, identified as 'Robert Codrell's tenement' which, by 1781 was operated by Thomas Lewis until 1799, when it seems to have been taken over by his son, John Lewis (senior), who worked the pottery until 1835 after which he was succeeded by his son, also named John, and later by his daughter Mary. During Mary's tenancy the pottery was worked by George Powell, son of another potter, Samuel Powell of Bolton (Messham 1956, 42). By the early 20th century the site was occupied by John Hughes.

A kiln and a range of buildings are shown on both the Lordship of Ewloe map of 1757 and the c.1780 Ewloe Estate map. The layout of the pottery appears unchanged by 1884, the mapping at that time also depicting a small square structure east of the pottery building and what is likely to be a waste dump some 60m to the west. A small pond is shown to the north of the pottery, positioned along a watercourse, associated with a well next to Willow Cottage, while a second stream or channel is shown to the south. Two rectangular features are located on the common, south of the pottery, which are likely to be clay pans, linked by another small watercourse. A small quantity of 19th-century pottery and kiln furniture was found on the edge of the common opposite the site in January 1975 (Davey 1976a, 21).

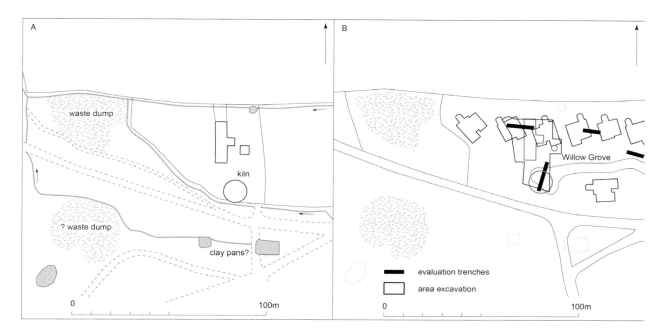

Figure 42 Site 5, Thomas Lewis' Pottery. A – detail from the Ordnance Survey mapping of 1884; B – present day showing the 2000 excavations and the location of pottery features in grey.

An evaluation, which included a geophysical survey, was conducted in March 2000 in advance of a housing development. This was followed in the summer by more detailed excavation which identified the well-preserved remains of a brick-built pottery kiln with a circular firing chamber and six flues radiating outwards from it, the whole being surrounded by a shade or hovel kiln (see Figure 16). The foundation of the main pottery building was also uncovered (see Figure 17), together with a number of intercutting pits, the site as a whole preserving a good stratigraphic sequence. The pottery recovered during the evaluation suggests production of mostly glazed, coarse earthenware vessels and finer blackware vessels, such as cups, from at least the mid-18th century onwards. Production of other pottery types, in particular slipwares, seems almost certainly to have taken place and the production of finer wares is also implied by the presence of a single sherd from a white salt-glazed stoneware waster (Earthworks 2000; Dodd 2003).

Events

Geophysical survey 2000 (PRN 118705; GeoQuest 2000)
Evaluation 2000 (PRN 123659; Earthworks 2000)
Excavation 2000 (PRN 129928; Dodd 2003)

Status

Unscheduled

Condition

The majority of the site now lies beneath a housing development, although this has not necessarily destroyed much of the buried remains.

Potential

Despite the construction of the housing estate there is significant potential for the survival of buried remains. The site of the kiln lies beneath the turning area at the end of the access road, while much of the main building lies beneath a drive. The site of the waste dump appears to be undisturbed, lying in an area of trees and scrub, while the possible clay pans, located on the common, are also likely to survive.

Associated records

PRN 123663 pottery complex
PRN 123664 kiln
PRN 123665 kiln
PRN 123666 pottery workshop
PRN 123667 17th/18th-century features

References

Davey 1976a, 21
Dodd 2003
Earthworks 2000
1757 Lordship of Ewloe map
1780 (circa) Ewloe Estate (Map XII)
1884 Ordnance Survey 1st edition 25" map

Buckley Potteries Site 6, Benjamin Davies' Pottery

PRN 101669
SJ 2763 6519
Date: 18th century

The pottery is depicted on the 1757 lordship of Ewloe map, showing one, or possibly two kilns and a rectangular building located on the common near the Pinfold crossroads. The c.1780 Ewloe Estate maps clearly show the kiln and a building immediately west of the pinfold itself, and the accompanying schedule lists the tenant as Benjamin Davies.

It had previously been thought that the site lay further to the east, in an area where a small quantity of 18th-century pottery was found during excavations for a septic tank (Davey 1976a, 21).

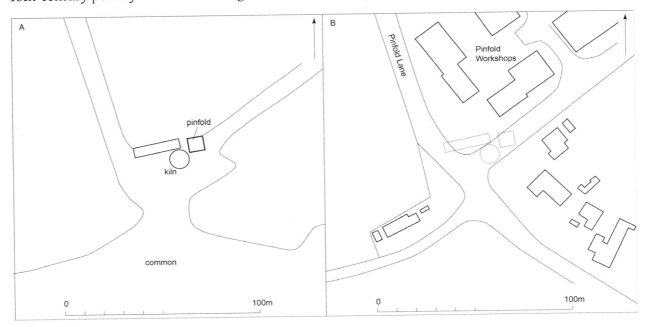

Figure 43 Site 6, Benjamin Davies' Pottery. A – detail from the Ordnance Survey mapping of 1884; B – present day showing the location of pottery features in grey.

Events

None

Status

Unscheduled

Condition

The area has been redeveloped and a road built over the site of the kiln, while the building is potentially located in an undeveloped corner of the area now occupied by the Pinfold Workshops.

Potential

It is possible that buried remains survive relating to the pottery building and perhaps other structures.

Associated records

PRN 97995 Pinfold

References

Davey 1976a, 21
1757 Lordship of Ewloe map
1780 (circa) Ewloe Estate (Map XII)

Buckley Potteries Site 7, Prescot's Pottery

PRN 101668
SJ 2776 6511
Date: 1783-1806

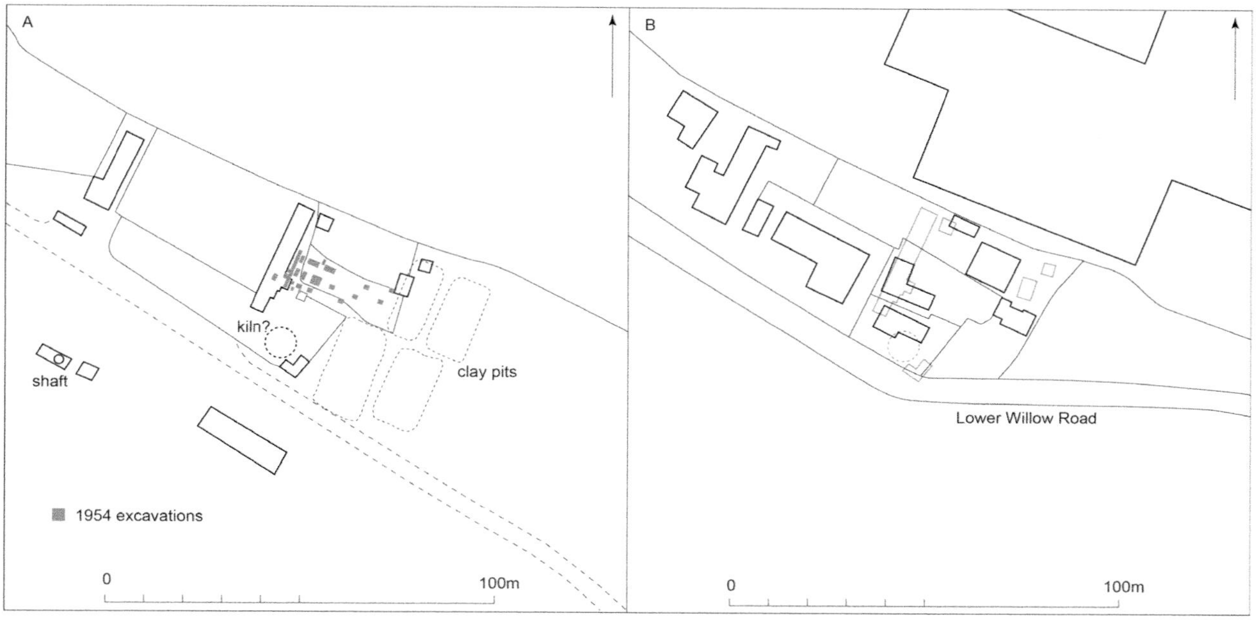

Figure 44 Site 7, Prescot's Pottery. A – detail from the Ordnance Survey mapping of 1884, showing the location of the 1954 excavations; B – present day showing the location of pottery features in grey.

Bartholomew Prescot built a pottery on a new encroachment on the common, which was in operation for just over twenty years between 1783 and 1806 (Messham 1956, 41). The period of activity falls between the major map sources and consequently no plan of the site is known. However, the Ordnance Survey 1st edition 25" map does show a range of buildings, perhaps comprising cottages and the workshop, together with three small buildings. Although there is no direct evidence for the location of the kiln, it has been suggested that it lay alongside the road on the southern edge of the site.

About a third of the area thought to contain the pottery was investigated by Barton in 1954. The kiln site was not located and structural finds in general were inconclusive. Pottery and kiln furniture of the period c.1740-1803 were recovered and are now in the Grosvenor Museum (Davey 1976a, 22). The excavation plan also indicates the position of four clay pits on the south-east side of the pottery site (Barton 1956).

The major product of this largely 18th-century site was a red-bodied, highly-fired, black-glazed earthenware consisting for the most part of large kitchen or dairy storage vessels and coarse table-wares. The site also produced small quantities of other ceramics such as slip- and agate-bodied wares (Davey and Longworth 2001, 63-4).

Events

Excavation 1954 (PRN 13038; Barton 1956)

Status

Unscheduled

Condition

The site of the kiln may lie beneath a bungalow and recent extension, while the house behind could be part of the original row of cottages.

Potential

There is limited potential for surviving buried remains towards the rear of the site.

Associated records

None

References

Barton 1956
Davey 1976a, 22
Davey and Longworth 2001, 63-4
Messham 1956, 41

Buckley Potteries Site 8, Catherall's Pottery

PRN 101678
SJ 2786 6505
Date: 18th – late 19th century

Jonathan Catherall I (1689-1761) was a founder of the fire-brick industry, having bought land from his brother John and nephew Joseph, and establishing a brick works in the area which later became the Trap Brickworks. The 1757 Lordship of Ewloe survey identifies his lands as well as 'Jonathan Catrell's House and Intack', which was located on the common, close to a group of three kilns. His will of 1751 bequeaths

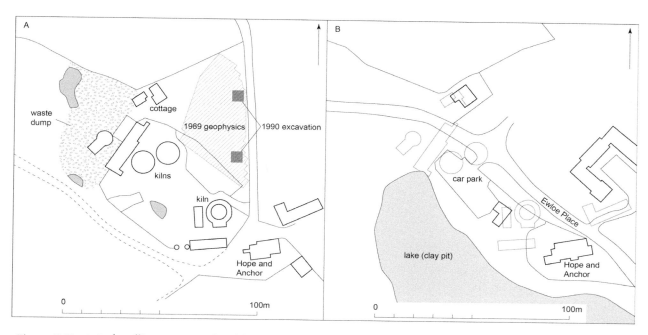

Figure 45 Site 8, Catherall's Pottery. A – detail from the Ordnance Survey mapping of 1884, showing the 1989-90 investigations; B – present day showing the location of pottery features in grey.

a pottery to his daughter Anne and her husband Edward Cunna, who had come to Ewloe to work for Catherall:

> 'my son in law Edward Conna of Ewloe, potter, has lately (by my permission but at his own expense) erected . . . an oven or pot-kiln . . . upon part of (my) freehold premises near to my dwelling house, where he now exercises the business of a potter . . . he shall have the said oven or pot-kiln for the (term of his) natural life and the life of his wife Anne Cunna'

The pottery was worked by Cunna until his death in 1782, after which his wife Anne continued until 1794; its subsequent fate is unknown (Messham 1956, 37). It is not clear, however, which pottery this refers to.

Following the death of Jonathan Catherall I the business of pottery and brickworks fell to his son John and then from 1777 to John's wife, Martha and their second son, Jonathan Catherall II, until her death in 1792. They appear to have rented two potteries, known as the large and small earthenware works (Messham notes two kilns, one for large and one for small wares), and lived as tenants at the Hope and Anchor adjacent to what may be presumed to be the larger of the works (Site 8). In 1786 Jonathan II built a stoneware works to export jars and bottles to Ireland for the spirit trade and in 1792 he married Catherine Jones, thereafter building a new home at Hawkesbury House.

The 1841 Tithe survey shows a range of buildings, including at least one kiln, while the Ordnance Survey 1st edition 25" mapping of 1884 shows three kilns with sundry other buildings, probable clay pans and a large waste dump on the west side. To the south-east of the complex is the Hope and Anchor public house, which was formerly the house of John Catherall. By the time of the 2nd edition of 1899 the pottery was disused and a large clay pit from an adjacent brick works had extended to take in the southern part of the pottery, including one of the kilns, while a second kiln had been lost to the construction of a new road which also cut through the waste dump.

Some elements of the pottery could still be identified as late as the mid-1970s, including a fine group of workers' terraces, while the sites of the kilns, sheds and chimneys could be seen as cropmarks next to the remains of an earlier potter's cottage. A stoneware flagon stamped Catherall, probably made at this site during the first quarter of the 19th century, is in the Grosvenor Museum, Chester (Davey 1976a, 22).

A watching brief by Earthworks Archaeology in 2002 found kiln furniture but appears not to have been within the area of the pottery itself (Earthworks 2002).

Events

Geophysical survey 1989 (PRN 70815; Gater and Gafney 1989)
Trial excavation 1990 (PRN 38549; Jones 1990)
Watching brief 2002 (PRN 110525; Earthworks 2002)

Status

Unscheduled

Condition

The majority of the pottery has been lost to clay extraction and redevelopment and the only visible trace is a worker's cottage on the north side of the road. The main pottery buildings could have preserved subsurface remains, although a new roundabout, car park and building are likely to have had a significant impact on the kiln bases.

Potential

There is limited potential for buried remains surviving between the northern end of the clay pit and the road.

Associated records

PRN 86732 possible kiln revealed by geophysics
PRN 86733 possible kiln revealed by geophysics

References

Davey 1976a, 22
Earthworks 2002
Gater and Gaffney 1989
Jones 1990
1841 Tithe Survey
1884 Ordnance Survey 1st edition 25"
1899 Ordnance Survey 2nd edition 25"

Buckley Potteries Site 9, Lamb's Pottery

PRN 101667
SJ 2824 6484
Date: late 18th century – 20th century

It is thought that the pottery might date from around 1740 and is certainly depicted on the 1757 map. In 1781 it was occupied by John Leach and in 1815 by Aaron Sharratt, who was born in Ewloe in 1751, his father (also Aaron) possibly having worked for Jonathan Catherall (the second). Sharratt set himself up as a master potter in 1800, presumably on this site, while in 1815 the pottery is recorded under the name of Anne Sharrat. Aaron had four sons, Aaron, Moses, Joshua and Jonathan, all potters, who continued the family business to the end of the 19th century.

The site of the pottery lies on the north-east side of Church Road and two kilns are shown on a map of 1860; these, together with several ranges of buildings are shown by the Ordnance Survey in 1875, the

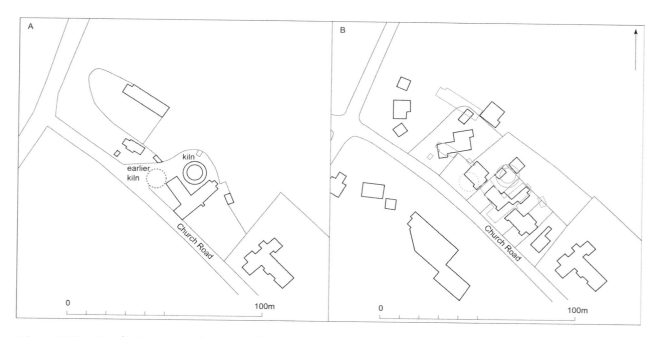

Figure 46 Site 9, Lamb's Pottery. A – detail from the Ordnance Survey mapping of 1875; B – present day showing the location of pottery features in grey.

layout changing little by 1912. There are several photographs of Lamb's pottery around 1909, which it has been assumed are at this site, since the pottery was also re-opened by Lamb after the Second World War, although only one or two firings were produced (Messham 1956, 56). A small quantity of 18th-century pottery has been found on the site (Davey 1976a, 22).

Events

None

Status

Unscheduled

Condition

The site of the kilns is now occupied by modern housing and driveways. One potter's cottage still survives on the opposite side of the road. The blunging pits were probably also on this side of the road. The site is now occupied by a petrol station.

Potential

There is little potential for surviving remains, perhaps with the exception of part of a kiln in the garden behind 134 Church Road.

Associated records

None

References

Davey 1976a, 22
Davey and Longworth 2001
Dodd 2017

McGarva 2000, 49, 86 and 102
Messham 1956, 56
1860 map of Buckley Estate
1875 Ordnance Survey 1st edition 25" map

Buckley Potteries Site 10, Hayes' Pottery

PRN 101666
SJ 2854 6474
Date: 18th – 1942

The pottery was first mapped in the 1780s, being occupied by Jonathan Hayes, although Messham records that the pottery had originally been occupied by Richard Dean until his death in 1763. From 1764 it was taken over by Joseph Hayes, the brother of Dean's widow Jane and father of Jonathan Hayes. Dean's son Philip was also a potter, and one of his two sons, John, also set up as a master potter in 1789 but died two years later (Messham 1956, 33-4). By 1809 the pottery was run by Jonathan Hayes's sister Phoebe and his son Joseph and in the early 20th century by Ollive Hayes. The pottery continued in the Hayes family until closing in 1942. There is a good photographic record of the pottery taken in 1960, copies of which are held at Flintshire Record Office, Hawarden.

There were two kilns here in 1860 and the Ordnance Survey 1st edition 25" map shows the kilns, together with a rectangular building which included the workshop and drying shed, with a small, rectangular pit on the opposite side of the road probably representing a soaking pit for preparing the clay. The later editions suggest that the pottery had been reduced to a single kiln, housed within a larger structure to which outbuildings were appended.

Events

None

Status

Unscheduled

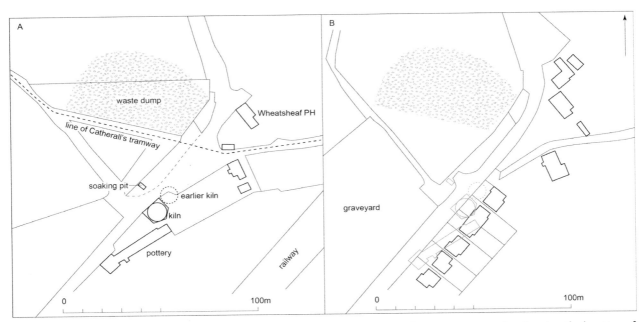

Figure 47 Site 10, Hayes' Pottery. A – detail from the Ordnance Survey mapping of 1875; B – present day showing the location of pottery features in grey.

Condition

The site of the kilns lies partly beneath the drives of modern houses and partly beneath the road, while the drying sheds are also beneath the houses and driveways. The waste dumps and blunging/soaking pits lie on the opposite side of the road, covered and somewhat obscured by trees and dense undergrowth (Davey 1976a, 23).

Potential

There is limited potential for the survival of the pottery structures themselves, although the waste dump appears to be undisturbed.

Associated records

None

References

Davey 1976a, 23
Davey and Longworth 2001, 63
Duckworth 1979
McGarva 2000, 10-11
Messham 1956, 33-4
1780 (circa) Ewloe Estate
1860 map of Buckley Estate
1875 Ordnance Survey 1st edition 25" map
1889 Ordnance Survey 2nd edition 25" map
1912 Ordnance Survey 3rd edition 25" map

Buckley Potteries Site 11, Price's Pottery

PRN 101677
SJ 2757 6462
Date: ?early 18th – mid 19th century

The 1757 Lordship of Ewloe map shows two rectangular buildings which equate with those of the pottery shown on the Ordnance Survey 1st edition 25" map of 1884, although no kiln is depicted to confirm this as a pottery at that time. A pottery is recorded here on the 1780s Ewloe Estate maps and appears to have been operational until the latter part of the 19th century, being disused by 1889.

The 1st edition mapping shows a single kiln and two buildings, as well as a small pond immediately to the north. The pottery was operated by Charles Price in the later 18th century and he was succeeded by his widow Martha and later his son Charles (Messham 1956, 34).

The site lies on the edge of the playing field of Elfed School and in 1974 works here to level the playing field led to considerable erosion of the pottery dump on its south and west sides. A quantity of 18th to 19th-century pottery and kiln furniture was recovered, including very fine mottled ware tankards (Davey 1976a, 23).

Small-scale community excavations were undertaken by CPAT in 2014-15 along the southern edge of the pottery, within the playing field associated with Elfed School (Hankinson and Culshaw 2014; Watson and Culshaw 2015). This demonstrated that landscaping has had a severe impact on the pottery dump and buried structural remains, although a significant quantity of wasters and kiln furniture was recovered.

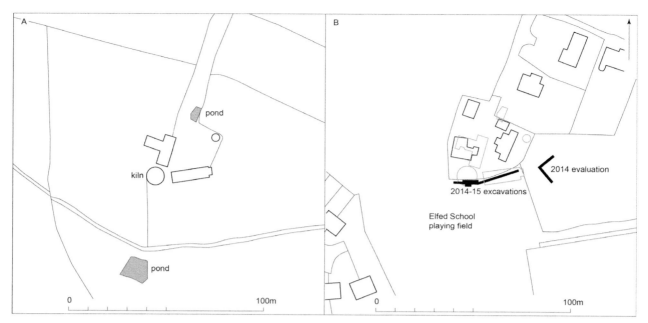

Figure 48 Site 11, Price's Pottery. A – detail from the Ordnance Survey mapping of 1884; B – present day showing the location of pottery features in grey.

An evaluation in 2014, in the field immediately to the east, revealed no evidence for any features associated with the pottery, but did recover a small collection of wasters dating from the 18th and 19th centuries (Hankinson and Jones 2014).

Events

1974 excavations (PRN 58481; Rutter 1977)
2014 excavations (PRN 128738; Hankinson and Culshaw 2014, 2015)
2014 evaluation (PRN 151548; Hankinson and Jones 2014)
2015 excavations (PRN 128739; Watson and Culshaw 2014)

Status

Unscheduled

Condition

One range of pottery buildings now lies under a modern house and the base of the kiln was demolished to erect a garage. The other range of buildings and the pottery dump were largely in the area of the playing fields, although landscaping has left little *in situ* evidence.

Potential

There is some potential for buried remains associated with the pottery structures to survive in the gardens around the house and garage, while the waste dump has been spread across the playing field.

Associated records

101677 duplicate record

References

Davey 1976a, 23
Hankinson 2014

Hankinson and Jones 2014
Hankinson and Culshaw 2014
Hankinson and Culshaw 2015
Messham 1956, 34
Rutter 1977
Watson and Culshaw 2014
1757 Lordship of Ewloe survey
1780 (circa) Ewloe Estate
1884 Ordnance Survey 1st edition 25" map
1889 Ordnance Survey 2nd edition 25" map

Buckley Potteries Site 12, Whitley's Pottery

PRN 101676
SJ 2785 6481
Date: 18th – 19th century

The 1757 Lordship of Ewloe map shows an enclosure here with a building at its northern end, although there is no indication of a kiln. The 1780s mapping, however, shows a single kiln located on the common, adjacent to the building, recording the plot as being occupied by Edward Whitely (house, garden and mug-kiln), who died in 1782. By 1815 the pottery was run by Robert Whitely, who died in 1826. The names Mary Whitely and John Whitely appear in the clay accounts for 1783-1789 and 1783-4 respectively (Messham 1956, 56), perhaps indicating that they were operating the pottery after the death of Edward. The pottery had may have fallen out of use by the 1840s as no kiln is depicted on the tithe survey, though this and the 1884 the Ordnance Survey mapping do show the main pottery building and several adjacent structures. To the west are two clay pits and what may be a clay pan, or perhaps a clay pit.

Events

None

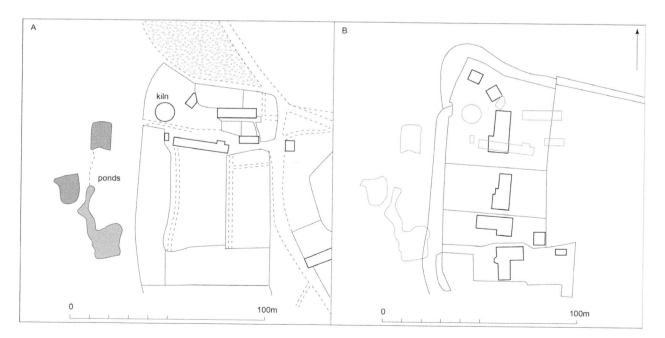

Figure 49 Site 12, Whitley's Pottery. A – detail from the Ordnance Survey mapping of 1884, with the approximate location of the kiln taken from a 1780s survey; B – present day showing the location of pottery features in grey.

Status

Unscheduled

Condition

The site of the main pottery building is occupied by a modern house while the kiln lies beneath the drive and the site of other buildings is within the garden. There is no visible trace of the clay pits and possible pan, which lie on the common, although buried remains may survive.

Potential

The potential for significant buried remains is limited and restricted to the foundations of ancillary structures which may survive within the garden area, together with features on the common which could potentially include the site of the waste dump.

Associated records

None

References

Davey 1976a, 24
Davey and Longworth 2001, 63
1757 Lordship of Ewloe survey
1780 (circa) Ewloe Estate
1875 Ordnance Survey 1st edition 25" map
1889 Ordnance Survey 2nd edition 25" map

Buckley Potteries Site 13, Buckley Common pottery

PRN 44489
SJ 2783 6482
Date: 19th century

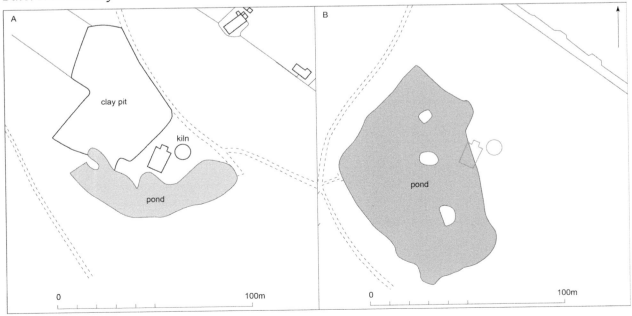

Figure 50 Site 13, Buckley Common Pottery. A – detail from the Ordnance Survey mapping of 1875; B – present day showing the location of pottery features in grey.

Little is known about this potential pottery which first appears on map sources in 1860, having been established on the open common. The Ordnance Survey 1st edition 25" map of 1875 shows a single kiln and an adjacent building surrounded by clay pits which appear to be too large for a small pottery, perhaps suggesting that the site was a brick works rather than a pottery.

Events

None

Status

Unscheduled

Condition

The dumping of up to 3m of soil in the landscaping of the Upper Common has obscured any trace of the site (Davey 1976a, 24).

Potential

Unknown

References

Davey 1976a, 24
Davey and Longworth 2001
1875 Ordnance Survey 1st edition 25" map

Buckley Potteries Site 14, Hancock's Pottery

PRN 101665
SJ 2845 6392
Date: c.1790-1886

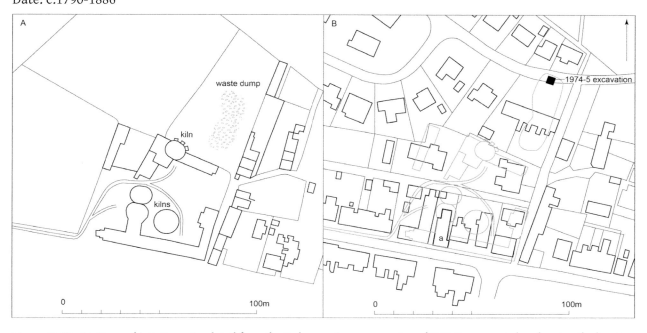

Figure 51 Site 14, Hancock's Pottery. A – detail from the Ordnance Survey mapping of 1875; B – present day showing the location of pottery features in grey and the site of the 1974-5 excavation.

Hancock's pottery, known as the Daisy Hill Works, was built in the late 18th century on land bought by Rigby and Hancock, occupying an existing enclosure on the commons, and is the only one of the Buckley potteries in the parish of Mold. It was founded by William Hancock whose mother was the daughter of the first Jonathan Catherall. In partnership with John Rigby, an ironmaster, Hancock founded the brick and colliery company of Rigby and Hancock in 1792, and later the pottery firm of William Hancock and Company, in partnership with William Williamson. Although their partnership was dissolved in 1817 the firm continued as one of the main brick and pottery concerns in Buckley throughout the 19th century (Messham 1956, 39-40).

Hancocks was the only pottery to be furnished with a purpose-built tramway, constructed in partnership with Rigby, which enabled the ready transportation of pottery, as well as bricks and coal, to the River Dee at Aston (Messham 1956, 39-40). The tramway is shown on the 1st edition Ordnance Survey 25" map of 1875 leading directly into the pottery complex, which then appears to have consisted of perhaps three kilns within a yard surrounded on two sides by pottery buildings. The waste dump is depicted to the north of the site and a small excavation was conducted towards its northern end in 1974-75 by Flintshire Historical Society, Chester Archaeology Society and the Buckley Society, directed by Davey and Williams, recovering a large quantity of domestic and industrial pottery and stoneware (Davey 1976a, 25). This also demonstrated that the dump extended further to the north than shown by the Ordnance Survey.

The peak production was around 1803 followed by a general decline, closing in 1886. The two major production types were vessels for the lead industry and domestic cooking and storage vessels. The domestic wares were black-glazed and slipware storage vessels and bowls, black- and brown-glazed fineware and stoneware (Davey and Longworth 2001, 62-72).

Events

Excavation 1974-5 (PRN 129929; Davey 1976a, 25)

Status

Unscheduled

Condition

The site of the kilns and other pottery buildings is now occupied by the former Catholic Church, shops, modern houses and gardens. A long timber building associated with the church lies on the site of one of the kilns. The only obvious surviving remains are of a small stone-built building on Brunswick Road which has been incorporated into a later building, now a funeral director's (labelled 'a' on Figure 51). This may have been the pottery office referred to by Davey (1976, 25). The dump lies beneath a 20th-century terrace, with the northern part occupied by gardens.

Potential

Despite the scale and significance of the pottery the potential is very limited, a result of its position in the centre of Buckley. There is, however, potential for remains relating to one of the kilns which may survive beneath a timber building, as well as the northern end of the waste dump, which is beneath gardens.

Associated records

None

References

Bentley 1973
Davey 1976a, 25

Davey 1976d
Davey and Longworth 2001
Longworth and McLaughlin Cook 2000
Messham 1956, 39-40
Philpot 1978
1875 Ordnance Survey 1st edition 25" map

Buckley Potteries Site 15, Powell's Pottery or Ewloe Pottery

PRN 101675
SJ 2741 6501
Date: late 19th – early 20th century

None of the early map sources suggests a pottery at this site, although an 18th-century pottery existed further to the south (Site 24), the earliest record here being in 1860, when two kilns are depicted. The pottery is named as Ewloe Pottery by the Ordnance Survey in 1884 and was operated by the Powell family. Messham (1956, 55) suggests that prior to the Powells the pottery was worked by the Lewis family, although the source of this information is unclear.

In the 1880s the pottery comprised a single kiln with a range of buildings to the west, as well as numerous small features which are likely to include clay pans, perhaps as many as three circular blungers and large clay pits to the north and west. By the end of the century the works had expanded, with the kiln site incorporated into a large complex of buildings.

During the 1970s the site was occupied by an industrial complex with the drying sheds having been incorporated into it, although no other visible traces of the pottery survived and the waste dump had been almost completely removed (Davey 1976a, 25).

A rapid archaeological evaluation, comprising four trenches, was undertaken during November 2003 prior to the commencement of a residential development. The results revealed the well-preserved base of a post-medieval pottery kiln, of probable multi-flued 'bottle-oven' type. The survival of the kiln suggests that other buildings and kilns, shown on early maps, may also survive within the immediate area, lying immediately below the modem ground level (Earthworks 2003).

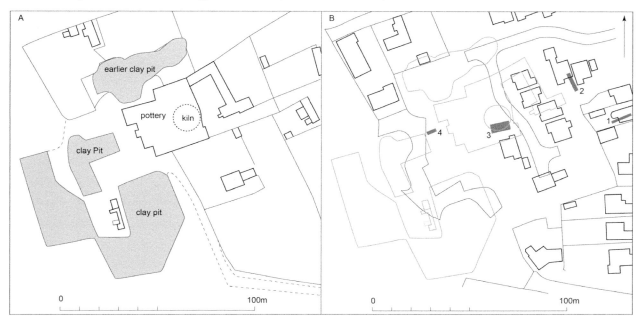

Figure 52 Site 15, Powell's Pottery. A – detail from the Ordnance Survey mapping of 1912; B – present day showing the location of pottery features in grey and the position of the 2004 excavations (1-4).

Events

Excavation 2003 (PRN 112379; Earthworks 2003)

Status

Unscheduled

Condition

The site is now occupied by a housing estate, although the position of the kiln and at least part of the main building complex lies within a green space in the centre of the development.

Potential

The 2004 excavation demonstrated that there is significant potential for buried remains to survive relating to the kiln and main complex and these have hopefully been preserved within the layout of the development.

Associated records

PRN 115573 Buckley, Pentre Lane, Potter's Cottage
PRN 126527 Ewloe Pottery, tank
PRN 128085 Buckley Potteries, Ewloe Pottery 18th-century phase
PRN 128159 Buckley Potteries, Ewloe pottery kiln
PRN 128160 Buckley Potteries, clay extraction pit

References

Davey 1976a, 25
Davey and Longworth 2001
Earthworks 2003
Messham 1956, 55
1860 map of Buckley Estate
1875 Ordnance Survey 1st edition 25" map
1889 Ordnance Survey 2nd edition 25" map

Buckley Potteries Site 16, Ledsham's Pottery

PRN 44490
SJ 2839 6460
Date: 18th century

A kiln and a range of buildings are depicted on the 1757 Ewloe Lordship map, the adjacent enclosures being described as 'Peter Ledsham's house garden and croft', and the 1780 Ewloe Estate map, which makes specific reference to a mug-kiln, but they do not appear on any 19th-century mapping.

Events

None

Status

Unscheduled

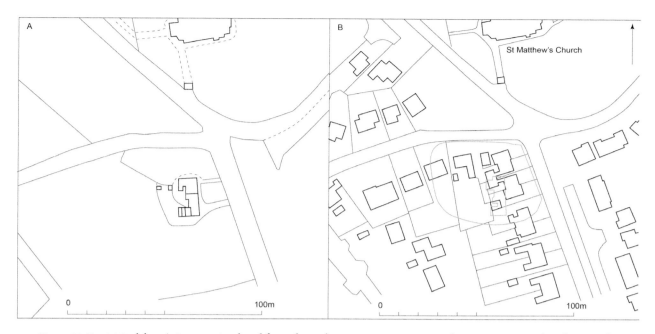

Figure 53 Site 16, Ledsham's Pottery. A – detail from the Ordnance Survey mapping of 1875; B – present day showing the location of the 19th-century building and possible extent of the pottery in grey.

Condition

There are no visible remains of the pottery, the whole being covered by modern houses and gardens (Davey 1976a, 27).

Potential

The potential for surviving buried remains is low, being restricted to garden plots which could conceivably contain parts of the pottery building and waste dump.

Associated records

PRN 98344, Mug kiln and croft, 1757

References

Davey 1976a, 27
Davey and Longworth 2001
1757 Lordship of Ewloe survey
1780 (circa) Ewloe Estate

Buckley Potteries Site 17, Ewloe Green Pottery

PRN 58480
SJ 2806 6633
Date: 1850 – 1914

According to Messham (1956, 55) the Ewloe Green pottery was started about 1850 by Hayes and Company and the 1860 Gwasaney clay accounts have a record for Hayes and Lathom, while an 1886 postal directory lists Jones and Jarrard (Gerrard), who continued in production until the First World War. William Jones and Charles Gerrard had a single kiln using clay from behind Oak's Farm on Pinfold Lane (Pritchard 2006, 80).

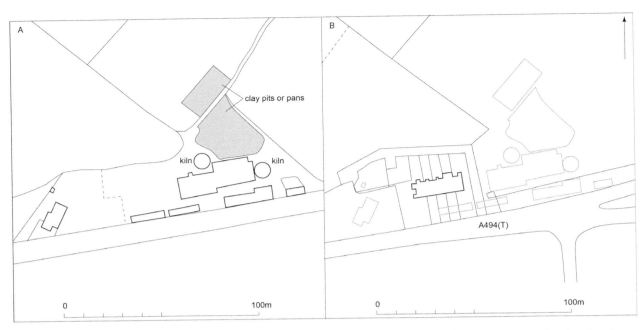

Figure 54 Site 17, Ewloe Green Pottery. A – detail from the Ordnance Survey mapping of 1874; B – present day showing the location of pottery features in grey.

The Ordnance Survey 1st edition 25" map of 1874 shows a range of buildings which presumably incorporated the kiln, since no separate kiln is depicted, together with two 'mills' and two ponds, or perhaps clay pans. By the end of the century further buildings had been added along the roadside and the main works expanded, while the mills had disappeared.

Events

None

Status

Unscheduled

Condition

The site of the main pottery complex lies in a pasture field within which there are slight earthworks indicating in part the position of the main buildings. Associated buildings along the roadside have been disturbed by road widening, although buried remains may still survive beneath the verge and along the edge of the field.

Potential

There is considerable potential for surviving buried structures relating to the main complex.

Associated records

None

References

Davey 1976a, 27
Davey and Longworth 2001
Longworth and McLaughlin Cook 2000, 55-6

Messham 1956, 55
Pritchard 2006, 80
1874 Ordnance Survey 1st edition 25" map
1889 Ordnance Survey 2nd edition 25" map
1912 Ordnance Survey 3rd edition 25" map

Buckley Potteries Site 18, Ewloe medieval pottery

PRN 44492
Date: medieval

The site of a medieval pottery kiln has been identified from a finds scatter discovered in 1975 by H M Harrison (Davey and Longworth 2001, 63). Over 1000 sherds of medieval pottery, including wasters, were discovered while fieldwalking an arable field, including 938 sherds of pottery and 161 ridge tile sherds. The main fabrics are gritty, highly fired white and grey wares with green and brown glazes. The major products were jugs, large storage vessels and roofing tiles, probably of 14/15th-century date (Figure 2a; Davey 1976a, 27).

A geophysical survey was undertaken in 1986, centred at SJ 2805 6565, and this was followed by a small excavation, comprising one main trench, measuring 12m by 3m, and two smaller trenches, each measuring 3m by 3m. The trenches had been positioned to investigate anomalies detected by the geophysics, although these proved to relate to ferrous objects and no evidence was forthcoming for the kiln or any other pottery structures. The topsoil produced quantities of pottery, including one sherd of 13th/14th-century pottery, 60 sherds of 14th/15th-century pottery, 146 sherds of 16th-century pottery and some 500 sherds of 18th/19th-century pottery (Weetman 1986).

Further geophysical survey was undertaken by CPAT in January 2015, covering a wider area than the previous survey, although again no obvious evidence was identified for kilns or any other archaeologically significant features (Hankinson 2015). However, it appears that the site of the original discovery may have been in the field to the north of the 1986 investigations, which was not covered by either the work in 1986 or the 2015 survey (Paul Davies, Buckley Society, pers comm.).

Event

Fieldwalking 1975
Geophysical survey (PRN 38251; Wheetman *1986*)
Excavation (PRN 129930; Wheetman 1986)
Geophysical survey (PRN 151547; Hankinson 2015)

Status

Unscheduled

Condition

The area where the sherds were found lies within a pasture field which contains some surface irregularities, although these are likely to relate to post-medieval industrial activity.

Potential

The site has perhaps the greatest potential of all the known Buckley potteries, being not only one of the earliest, but is also apparently undisturbed.

Associated records

PRN 102717 finds scatter

Figure 55 Site 18 showing the location of the 1986 geophysical and trial excavations.

References

Davey 1976a, 27
Davey and Longworth 2001
Hankinson 2015
Harrison and Davey 1975
Harrison and Davey 1977
Maude 1986
Wheetman 1986

Buckley Potteries Site 19, Pinfold Lane Pottery

PRN 101679
SJ 2745 6638
Date: 17th – 18th century

The site was discovered in 1975 during excavations for an electricity cable which exposed a layer of coal ash and clinker 0.2m thick extending for 10m and three pits full of kiln wasters. Finds included black-glazed wares and thrown, flanged bowls with yellow slip trailed decoration, probably dating to 1650-80. A derelict stone cowshed 3m north of the trench is a re-used cottage with a fireplace which may have been the potter's cottage. Irregularities in the pasture to the north may reflect other pottery structures (Davey 1976a, 28).

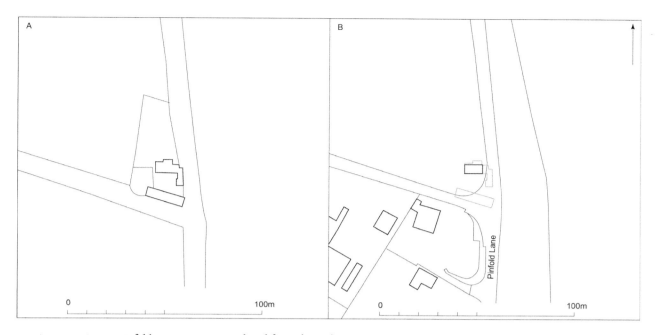

Figure 56 Site 19, Pinfold Lane Pottery. A – detail from the Ordnance Survey mapping of 1874; B – present day showing the location of pottery features in grey.

The cottage is depicted on 1757 and 1780s map sources, although there is no indication that this was then a pottery.

Events

None

Status

Unscheduled

Condition

The remains of the cottage are in a poor condition, while the immediate area is overgrown.

Potential

There is the potential for significant buried remains in the area immediately surrounding the cottage, although further to the west the land has been quarried.

Associated records

None

References

Davey 1976a, 28
Davey 1976b
Davey and Longworth 2001
Longworth and McLaughlin Cook 2000, 45-50
Morgan 1978
1757 Lordship of Ewloe survey
1780 (circa) Ewloe Estate

Buckley Potteries Site 20, Benjamin Catherall's Pottery

PRN 128081
SJ 2814 6490
Date: 18th century

A map of the lordship of Ewloe in 1757 shows three kilns - two on Benjamin Catrell's Land and one on the edge of the common, together with a rectangular building. The accompanying schedule lists this as 'Benjamin Catrell's claypits and garden'. No pottery is recorded here on any later mapping. Benjamin was the nephew of the first Jonathan Catherall and owned land adjoining his, both Catheralls being pottery and brick manufacturers. The two branches of the family had widely differing fortunes, Benjamin appearing to be in constant debt (Messham 1956, 36-7). He died in 1801 and there is no subsequent record of a pottery at this site. He was also associated with the pottery on Pinfold Lane (Site 2) during the same period.

Events

None

Status

Unscheduled

Condition

The site is now occupied by modern housing, gardens and a carpark.

Potential

It is possible that some sub-surface remains survive, although the overall potential is considered to be low.

Associated records

None

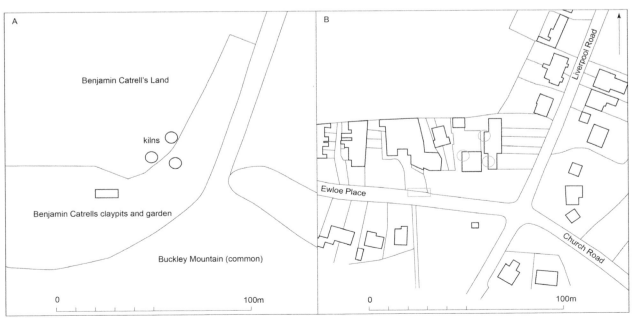

Figure 57 Site 20, Benjamin Catherall's Pottery. A – detail from the 1757 estate map showing the approximate position of structures; B – present day showing the location of pottery features in grey.

References

1757 Lordship of Ewloe survey

Buckley Potteries Site 21

PRN 128082
SJ 286 652
Date: early 19th century

A pottery is recorded on the 1834 Ordnance Survey Surveyors' Drawing in approximately the location later occupied by the Etna Brickworks.

Events

None

Status

Unscheduled

Condition

Unknown

Potential

Unknown

Associated records

None

References

1834 Ordnance Survey Surveyors' Drawing

Buckley Potteries Site 22, Church Road Pottery

PRN 128083
SJ 285 643
Date: early 19th century

A pottery is recorded on the 1834 Ordnance Survey Surveyors' Drawing, although the precise location is unclear.

Events

None

Status

Unscheduled

Condition

Unknown

Potential

Unknown

Associated records

None

References

1834 Ordnance Survey Surveyors' Drawing

Buckley Potteries Site 23, Lane End Pottery

PRN 128084
SJ 290 639
Date: early 19th century

A pottery is recorded on the 1834 Ordnance Survey Surveyors' Drawing, although the exact location is unclear. However, a map of 1815 records a 'kiln field' with the owner or tenant as Joseph Saladine.

Events

None

Status

Unscheduled

Condition

Unknown

Potential

Unknown

Associated records

None

References

1815 Survey of the Township of Pentrobin
1834 Ordnance Survey Surveyors' Drawing

Buckley Potteries Site 24

PRN 128085
SJ 2744 6494
Date: 18th century

A pottery is depicted on the 1757 Lordship of Ewloe map, showing a single kiln and a rectangular building on the common, south of the site of the 19th-century Ewloe, or Powell's Pottery. According to Messham

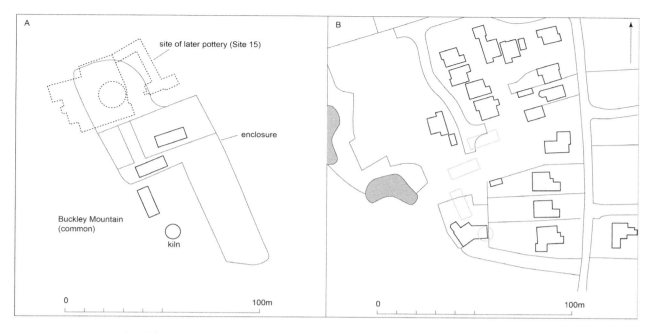

Figure 58 Site 24. A – detail from the 1757 estate map showing the approximate position of structures; B – present day showing the location of pottery features in grey.

(1956, 55) Powell established a pottery on a site formerly worked by the Lewis family, who may therefore have run this pottery, although the enclosures on this part of the common appear to have been associated with Peter Ledsham in 1757 and Benjamin Davies in the 1780s, both potters with known sites elsewhere (Site 16 and 6 respectively).

Events

None

Status

Unscheduled

Condition

The exact location of the kiln is not known, and the area has recently been redeveloped as a housing estate.

Potential

Despite the redevelopment there remains some potential for the survival of buried structures within the garden plots.

Associated records

None

References

Messham 1956, 55
1757 Lordship of Ewloe survey

Buckley Potteries Site 25, Charles Cunnah's Pottery

PRN 128086
SJ 2875 6718
Date: 18th century

The Ewloe Estate map of *c.* 1780 has a later schedule dated 1804 which lists 'Work House Field Mug Kiln', a tenement in the occupation of Charles Cunnah, the same details also being recorded in 1815. No buildings are shown on either map, or on the 1757 map. However, the 1815 map shows no pottery in this field but does depict a building further to the east, now Castle Bank Cottage (PRN 99013), where there is a record of clay pipes found within the garden and an old tip in the field behind. Although a building (now demolished) is depicted along the roadside by the Ordnance Survey in 1871, this is too late to be associated with the pottery. The site lies somewhere in a pasture field within which there is a level area which could have been the site of the pottery, together with an obvious linear hollow further to the east, aligned north-north-east to south-south-west, that is perhaps unlikely to have been associated with the pottery.

Events

None

Status

Unscheduled

Condition

The exact location of the pottery remains uncertain and its condition is therefore unknown.

Potential

The undeveloped nature of the site suggests that there is considerable potential for the survival of buried remains which could be elucidated through geophysical survey, while a programme of fieldwalking might also shed some light on the position and extent of the pottery, as well as the types of wares it produced.

Associated records

None

References

1780 (circa) Ewloe Estate (Map XI) and   1804 schedule
1815 Survey of the Township of Ewloe Wood

Buckley Potteries Site 26, Hawarden Hayes

PRN 128087
SJ 3096 6536
Date: early 19th century

A pottery was recorded in 1815 near Hawarden Hayes, the schedule noting 'pot kiln and works', owned and occupied by William Boydell, while the fields to the south evidently contained clay pits, one field also noted as 'pantile field'. According to Messham (1956, 61) the pottery was operated by a Mr Smalley, a member of a cotton spinning family from Holywell, who also established a brick works near Hayes' pottery. The precise location is difficult to determine but now lies under grass within a golf course.

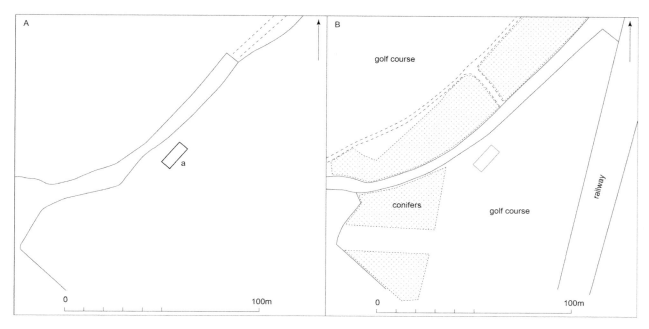

Figure 59 Site 26. A – detail from the Ordnance Survey mapping of 1870 showing the approximate position of the building (a) depicted in 1815; B – present day showing the approximate location of pottery features in grey.

Events

None

Status

Unscheduled

Condition

There is no visible evidence and the site may have been impacted upon by landscaping for the golf course.

Potential

The site may have significant potential for the preservation of buried remains.

Associated records

None

References

Messham 1956, 61
1815 survey of the Township of Ewloe Town

Buckley Potteries Site 27, Wilson's Pottery

PRN 128089
SJ 2800 6495
Date: 1915

A short-lived pottery was started at Ewloe Place in May 1915 by Ernest Wilson, although Rice Jones is recorded as the potter (Pritchard 2006, 80). The exact location of the pottery is not known.

Events

None

Status

Unscheduled

Condition

Unknown

Potential

Unknown

Associated records

None

References

Pritchard 2006, 80

Buckley Potteries Site 28, Trap Pottery

PRN 128090
SJ 278 653
Date: 1918

A short-lived pottery is recorded at the Trap in 1918 (Pritchard 2006, 80), although the exact location is not known.

Events

None

Status

Unscheduled

Condition

There are no surface remains, although the site is likely to have well-preserved, buried remains.

Potential

The site lies in a pasture field and has significant potential for the preservation of buried remains.

Associated records

None

References

Pritchard 2006, 80

Buckley Potteries Site 29, Dirty Mile Pottery

PRN 128091
SJ 3004 6315
Date: 1918

A short-lived pottery is recorded along the Dirty Mile (Pritchard 2006, 80), the location of which is perhaps indicated by the identification of 'kiln field' on a map of 1915 (D/BJ/346), owned by Edward Lewis, and lying to the west of Bannel Lane. The adjacent field to the west contained clay pits. There is no visible trace of the pottery and although the adjacent field to the north-east does contain some slight earthworks these are not necessarily related.

Events

None

Status

Unscheduled

Condition

Unknown

Potential

Unknown

Associated records

None

References

Pritchard 2006, 80

Buckley Potteries Site 30, Welsh Art Pottery

PRN 128092
SJ 288 638
Date: 1914-16

Frederick James Holloday's Welsh Art Pottery Company operated along Chester Road, Buckley, from February 1914 to November 1916 (Pritchard 2006, 80), although the exact location is not known.

Events

None

Status

Unscheduled

Condition

Unknown

Potential

Unknown

Associated records

None

References

Pritchard 2006, 80

Buckley Potteries Site 31, Alltami Pottery

PRN 128094
SJ 2656 6549
Date: 1915

INSERT [Figure 60 Site 31, Alltami Pottery. A – detail from the Ordnance Survey mapping of 1912, showing approximate position of pottery (a) and kiln (b); B – present day showing the location of pottery features in grey.]

A pottery is depicted on a map of 1915 (D/DM/578/47), showing a rectangular building with a single kiln to the east. The pottery was presumably short-lived, and no further details are known.

Events

None

Status

Unscheduled

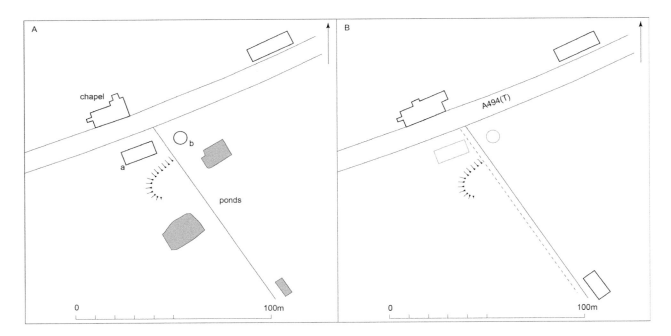

Figure 60 Site 31, Alltami Pottery. A – detail from the Ordnance Survey mapping of 1912, showing approximate position of pottery (a) and kiln (b); B – present day showing the location of pottery features in grey.

Condition

There are slight earthworks defining a hollow which may have been the pottery building and if so the kiln could have been in the adjacent field to the east.

Potential

Unknown

Associated records

None

References

Pritchard 2006, 80
1915 Plan of Buckley and district

Bibliography

NMGM refers to National Museums and Galleries Merseyside (Liverpool)

Allan, J. P., 1984. *Medieval and post-medieval finds from Exeter.* Exeter: Exeter City Council and University of Exeter.

Amery, C. A., 1979. *An inventory of sgraffito ware from Brookhill, Buckley, Clwyd (Site 1).* Unpublished. Flintshire Record Office, Hawarden MSS, NT/607. [Site 1: *Buckley Archive* NMGM, I, 43, 11/1-5]

Amery, A. and Davey, P. J., 1979. Post-medieval pottery from Brookhill, Buckley, Clwyd (Site 1), *Medieval and Later Pottery in Wales* **2**: 49-85.

Axworthy Rutter, J. A., 1990. Other finds from the Dominican Friary: pottery in S. W. Ward *Excavations at Chester: the lesser religious houses, sites investigated 1964-1983.* Chester: Chester City Council, 138-163.

Barton, K. J., 1956. The Buckley Potteries II. Excavations at Prescot's Pottery 1954. *Publications of the Flintshire Historical Society* 16: 63-87.

Bentley, J., 1973. *Hancock's Pottery site finds.* Unpublished. [Site 14: *Buckley Archive* NMGM, III, 52, 3/1; 10 A4 pages]

Bentley, J., 1976a. *Investigation of possible kiln sites at Brookhill.* Unpublished. Flintshire Record Office, Hawarden. Unpublished. MSS BP 1243. [Site 1: *Buckley Archive* NMGM, I, 25, 5/1/6-11]

Bentley, J., 1976b. *Excavations of a possible kiln site at Brookhill Buckley. Part 2, between July and December 1976 'The Waster Pit'.* Unpublished. Flintshire Record Office, Hawarden, MSS BP 1290. [Site 1: *Buckley Archive* NMGM, I, 26, 5/1/12-13]

Bentley, J., 1977a. *Excavation of a possible kiln site at Brookhill Buckley. Part 3, U3 and U4 Jan-May 1977.* Unpublished. Flintshire Record Office, Hawarden, MSS BP 1366. [Site 1: *Buckley Archive* NMGM, I, 26, 5/1/14-16]

Bentley, J., 1977b. *A post-medieval excavation at Brookhill Buckley (SJ 278655) October 1975 – August 1977.* Unpublished. Flintshire Record Office, Hawarden, MSS NT/604. [Site 1: *Buckley Archive* NMGM, I, 26, 5/1/17-19]

Bentley, J., 1978a. *Exposure of further kiln sites at Brookhill Buckley SJ 278655 October 1977 – March 1978.* Unpublished. Flintshire Record Office, Hawarden, MSS NT/512. [Site 1: *Buckley Archive* NMGM, I, 26, 5/1/20-22]

Bentley, J., 1978b. *Further kiln traces, and observations on the kilns.* Unpublished. Flintshire Record Office, Hawarden, MSS NT/605. [Site 1: *Buckley Archive* NMGM, I, 26, 5/1/23-24]

Bentley, J., 1979a. *Observations on kiln furniture at Brookhill and Pinfold pottery excavations.* Unpublished. Flintshire Record Office, Hawarden, MSS NT/590. [Sites 1 and 2: *Buckley Archive* NMGM, I, 27, 5/3/1-3]

Bentley, J., 1979b. Correspondence relating to the excavations at Brookhill, Buckley. Unpublished. NT/606, Flintshire Record Office, Hawarden.

Bentley, J., 1979c. Buckley and its connection with the mercantile marine, *Buckley* 5, 11-14.

Bentley, J., 1982. An early pottery site in Buckley, *Buckley* 7, 8-14.

Bentley, J., 1984a. *Further examination of fire-hole at U3/4 BrC.* Unpublished. Flintshire Record Office, Hawarden, MSS NT/1310. [Site 1: *Buckley Archive* NMGM, I, 27, 5/3/7]

Bentley, J., 1984b. *Report up to date at Brookhill U3/4 area, BrC.* Unpublished. Flintshire Record Office, Hawarden, MSS NT/1309. [Site 1: *Buckley Archive* NMGM, I, 27, 5/3/15]

Bentley, J., 1984c. *Post-medieval kilns at Buckley.* Unpublished. [Site 1: *Buckley Archive* NMGM, I, 28, 5/3/6]

Bentley, J., 1985a. *'Saggar' types found at Brookhill and their use.* Unpublished. Flintshire Record Office, Hawarden, MSS NT/1308. [Site 1: *Buckley Archive* NMGM, I, 27, 5/3/8]

Bentley, J., 1985b. *Possible dating of certain pieces of Buckley scraffito pottery.* Unpublished. [Site 1: *Buckley Archive* NMGM, I, 28, 5/3/10]

Bentley, J., 1985c. *Further observations on kiln structure.* Unpublished. [Site 1: *Buckley Archive* NMGM, I, 28, 5/3/11]

Bentley, J., n.d. *Brookhill cinder area saggars and their dispersal, notable features of BrC.* Unpublished. [Site 1: *Buckley Archive* NMGM, I, 28, 5/3/9]

Bentley, J., Davey, P. J. and Harrison, M., 1979. Buckley clay tobacco pipes, *Buckley Journal* 5: 15-22.

Bentley, J., Davey, P. J. and Harrison, H. M., 1980. An early clay pipe industry in north Wales, in P. J. Davey (ed.) *The Archaeology of the Clay Tobacco Pipe III. Britain: the North and West.* British Archaeological Reports, British Series **78**: 273-82.

Bentley, J. and Harrison, H. M., 1973a. Pinfold Lane Pottery, Buckley, *Archaeology in Wales* 13: 61.

Bentley, J. and Harrison, H. M., 1973b. *Benjamin Cottrell's Pinfold Lane pottery, Buckley*. Unpublished. Logbook of Part 1 excavations 1972-73. [Site 2: *Buckley Archive* NMGM, II, 47, 3/1]

Bentley, J. and Harrison, H. M., 1974a. *Benjamin Cottrell's Pinfold Lane pottery, Buckley*. Unpublished. Logbook of Stage 2 excavations 1973-74. [Site 2: *Buckley Archive* NMGM, II, 47, 3/2]

Bentley, J. and Harrison, H. M., 1974b. *Preliminary excavations of a pottery site in Pinfold Lane, Buckley*. Unpublished. Flintshire Record Office, Hawarden, MSS NT/182. [Site 1: *Buckley Archive* NMGM, II, 47, 4/2]

Bentley, J. and Harrison, H. M., 1975a. *Buckley clay tobacco pipes from recent excavations*. Unpublished. Flintshire Record Office, Hawarden, MSS BP 1103. [*Buckley Archive* NMGM, I, 20, 4/3/1]

Bentley, J. and Harrison, H. M., 1975b. *Investigation of a possible pottery site*. Unpublished. Flintshire Record Office, Hawarden, MSS BP 1286. [Site 1: *Buckley Archive* NMGM, I, 25, 5/1/1-5]

Boyle, A., 2002-3. The Cistercian ware products of Ticknall, south Derbyshire, *Medieval Ceramics*: 26-27, 113-118.

Cook, J. M. and Longworth, C., 2000. *Buckley Archive*. Unpublished. National Museums and Galleries on Merseyside, Liverpool. [Finding aid for the Buckley archive material held by the Museum, 89 pages]

Crew, P., 2002. Melin Tyddyn Du drying kiln, Maentwrog, *Archaeology in Wales* 42: 81-84.

Crew, P., 2003. *Perforated tiles from grain drying kilns and malt kilns*. Unpublished. Plas Tan y Bwlch: Snowdonia National Park Study Centre. [5 A4 pages]

Campbell, S. D. G., and Hains, B. A., 1988. British Geological Survey Technical Report WA/88/2, Deeside (North Wales) thematic geological mapping. Keyworth: British Geological Survey.

Cropper, T., 1906. Early tobacco clay pipe making at Buckley, *The Cheshire Sheaf*, May 1906: 43-44.

Cropper, T., 1923. *Buckley and District*. Buckley: Cropper and Sons.

Davey, P. J., 1974. *The Buckley Potteries: an archaeological field report*. Buckley Clay Industries Research Committee, Flint (Revised 1975).

Davey, P. J., 1975a. *Buckley Pottery, Buckley Clay Industries Research Committee*.

Davey, P. J., 1975b. Recent work on the Buckley Potteries, *Journal of Post-Medieval Archaeology* **9**: 236-39.

Davey, P. J., 1976a. Recent fieldwork in the Buckley Potteries, *Buckley* 4: 16-29.

Davey, P. J., 1976b. Clwyd: Buckley (Flintshire) (SJ/274664), *Post-medieval Archaeology* 10: 174.

Davey, P. J., 1976c. Clwyd: Buckley (Flintshire), *Post-medieval Archaeology* 9: 257-258.

Davey, P. J., 1976d. *Hancock's Pottery (Buckley: Site 14)*. Unpublished. [Site 14: *Buckley Archive* NMGM, III, 52, 3/2]

Davey, P. J., 1981. Guidelines for the processing and publication of clay pipes from excavations, *Medieval and later pottery in Wales* 4: 65-88.

Davey, P. J., 1987. Further observations on a post-medieval kiln group from Pinfold Lane, Buckley, in B. Vyner and S. Wrathmell (eds) *Studies in medieval and later pottery in Wales presented to J. M. Lewis*. Cardiff: Department of Extra-Mural Studies, University College: 93-120.

Davey, P. J., Hughes, M. and Longworth, C., 2014. Portable X-ray fluorescence analysis of 18th-century black-glazed pottery. *Medieval Ceramics* 35: 62-72.

Davey, P. J. and Hodges, R. (eds), 1983. *Ceramics and Trade: The Production and Distribution of Later Medieval Pottery in North-West Europe*. Sheffield: University of Sheffield.

Davey, P. J. and Longworth, C. M., 2001a. The identification of Buckley pottery, *Archaeology in Wales* 41: 62-72.

Davey, P. J. and Longworth, C. M., 2001b. *300 years of Buckley Pottery: 1650-1950*. Unpublished. [Summary note prepared for the MPRG conference, Liverpool, 6th October 2001]

Davidson, L. S., 1982. Thin section analysis of clay used in five British clay pipe production centres', *The Archaeology of the Clay Tobacco Pipe* 7. Oxford: British Archaeological Reports, British Series 100: 311-344.

Davies, J. R., Wilson, D., and Williamson, I. T., 2004. *Geology of the country around Flint: Memoir for 1:50,000 Geological Sheet 108*. Keyworth: British Geological Survey.

Dodd, L. J., 2003. Excavations on the site of the Lewis pottery complex, Buckley, North Wales, United Kingdom, *Ceramics in America* 2003: 245-248.

Dodd L. J., 2017 *Land at 129 Church Road, Buckley, Flintshire (centring on NGR SJ 282 647): an archaeological strip, map and record exercise, Hawarden*. Unpublished Earthworks Archaeology, Report No E1340.

Duckworth, C., 1979. The story of nonconformity in Buckley and district. *Buckley* 5: 2-10.

Earthworks, 2000. *Proposed Residential Development on land off White Farm Road and The Willows, Buckley, Flintshire: a programme of archaeological evaluation*. Unpublished. Earthworks Archaeology E414.

Earthworks, 2002. *Proposed Housing Development on Land Opposite the Hope and Anchor Public House, Buckley, Flintshire: an archaeological watching brief*. Unpublished. Earthworks Archaeology E477.

Earthworks, 2003. *Residential Development at the Former Ewloe Pottery Site, Pentre Lane, Buckley, Flintshire. A Rapid Archaeological Evaluation.* Unpublished. Earthworks Archaeology E718.

Earthworks, 2005. *Land adjacent to Ivy Cottage, Alltami, Flintshire: an archaeological assessment.* Unpublished. Earthworks Archaeology, Report No E836.

Gater, J. A. and Gaffney, C., 1990. Report on Geophysical Survey, Buckley, Clwyd. Unpublished. Geophysical Surveys, Bradford.

GeoQuest, 2000a. Geophysical Survey of an area of land at White Farm Road, Buckley, Flintshire. Unpublished. GeoQuest Associates.

GeoQuest 2000b. *Archaeomagnetic Study of Hearth Context 104, Buckley, Flintshire.* Unpublished. GeoQuest Associates.

Frost, P., 2004. Buckley, Lane End Brickworks (SJ 289 640), *Archaeology in Wales* 44: 189.

Hankinson, R., 2014. Buckley, Price's Pottery (SJ 2757 6462), *Archaeology in Wales* 54: 223.

Hankinson, R., 2015. *Buckley Potteries, Site 18: geophysical survey.* Unpublished. CPAT Report No. 1321.

Hankinson, R., 2017. *Brookhill Pottery, Buckley: Archaeological Assessment,* Unpublished. CPAT Report No 1476.

Hankinson, R. and Culshaw, V., 2014. *Price's Pottery, Buckley, Flintshire: Archaeological Investigations 2014.* Unpublished. CPAT Report No. 1297.

Hankinson, R. and Jones, N. W., 2014. *Land to the rear of Withen Cottage, Alltami Road, Buckley: Archaeological evaluation.* Unpublished. CPAT Report No. 1274.

Hankinson, R. and Culshaw, V., 2015. Buckley, Price's Pottery (SJ 2757 6462), *Archaeology in Wales* 55: 68.

Harrison, H. M. and Davey, P. J., 1977. Ewloe kiln, in P. J. Davey (ed.), *Medieval Pottery from Excavations in the North West,* Liverpool, Institute of Extension Studies, 92-99.

Hartley, D., 1974. *Made in England,* 4th edition. London: Eyre Methuen.

Higgins, D. A., 1983. Clay tobacco pipes from Brookhill, Buckley, *Medieval and Later Pottery in Wales* **6:** 50-64.

Higgins, D. A., 1995. More pipes from the Bentley Collection, Buckley, Clwyd, *Society for Clay Pipe Research Newsletter* **46:** 9-13.

Jones, N. W., 1990. Pinfold Lane, Buckley, *Archaeology in Wales* 30: 70.

Jones, N. W., 2014. *The Buckley Potteries: an assessment of survival and potential.* Unpublished. CPAT Report No. 1246.

Knight, J., 2001. *Excavations at Pinfold Lane, Buckley.* Unpublished.

Lewis, S., 1833. *A Topographical Dictionary of Wales.* London: S. Lewis and Co.

Lloyd Gruffydd, K., 1970. Medieval coalmining in Flintshire, *Buckley* 1.

Lloyd Gruffydd, K., 1971. Coalmining in Flintshire in the sixteenth century, *Buckley* 3.

Lloyd Gruffydd, K., 1975. The Flintshire coalfield during the sixteenth and seventeenth centuries, *Buckley* 3.

Lloyd Gruffydd, K., 1980. Seventeenth-century bestiary ware from Buckley, Clwyd, *Archaeologia Cambrensis* 129: 160-165.

Longworth, C. M., 1999. *Buckley Sgraffito.* Unpublished M.Phil thesis, University of Liverpool.

Longworth, C. M., 2004. Buckley Sgraffito: a study of a 17th-century pottery industry in North Wales, its production techniques and design influences, *Internet Archaeology,* <http://intarch.ac.uk/journal/issue16/longworth_index.html>

Longworth, C., 2005. Buckley ceramics in the 17th century: socio-economic status of the potters and possible design influences, *Interpreting Ceramics* 6 <www.uwic.ac.uk/ICRC>

Longworth, C. and Davey, P., 2016. Terre cuite à glaçure tachetée britannique', 'Terre cuite à glaçure noire britannique', 'Terre cuite engobée et glaçurée britannique façonnée au tour' and 'Terre cuite engobée et glaçurée britannique mise en forme par moulage' in Métreau L (ed) *Identifier la céramique au Québec,* Québec: Centre interuniversitaire d'études sure les lettres, les arts et les traditions (CELAT): 129-132, 137-143, 161-166 and 167-171.

Longworth, C. and McLaughlin Cook, J., 2000. *Buckley Archive held in the National Museums & Galleries on Merseyside.* Unpublished manuscript.

Lyons, S., 1986. The organisation of the Buckley brick industry in the second half of the nineteenth century, *Buckley* 11: 34-42.

McCarthy, M. R. and Brooks, C. M., 1988. *Medieval pottery in Britain AD 900-1600.* Leicester: Leicester University Press.

Maude, K., 1986. *Magnetometer survey at Buckley, Clwyd.* Unpublished. Department of Archaeology, University of Manchester. [Site 18: *Buckley Archive* NMGM, IV, 55, 3/1]

McGarva, A., 2000. *Country Pottery. Traditional Earthenware of Britain.* London: A & C Black (Publishers) Ltd.

McNeil, R., 1984. *Pinfold Lane, Buckley AS31 1984.* Unpublished. Environmental Advisory Unit, University of Liverpool.

McNeil, R., 1985a. Excavations in Buckley, *Archaeology in Clwyd* 7: 20-21.

McNeil, R., 1985b. Clwyd: Buckley (Flintshire) SJ/275655, *Post-medieval Archaeology* 19: 180-181.

Messham, J. E., 1956. The Buckley potteries, *Flintshire Historical Society Publications* **16**: 31-61.

Messham, J. E., 1989. A Ewloe bailiff's account and the origins of the Buckley pottery industry, *Flintshire Historical Society Journal* 32: 167-175.

Miles, H., 1977. Rhuddlan, in P. J. Davey (ed.) *Medieval Pottery from Excavations in the North West*, Liverpool, Institute of Extension Studies: 60-61.

Moorhouse, S. and Roberts, I., 1992. *Wrenthorpe potteries: excavations of 16th and 17th-century potting tenements near Wakefield*. Wakefield: West Yorkshire Archaeology Service.

Morgan, D., 1978. *Buckley Site 19: a study of a possible early post-medieval pottery production site in Buckley, Clwyd* Unpublished Extra-mural Certificate in Archaeology dissertation, University of Liverpool. [Site 19: *Buckley Archive* NMGM, I, 42, 10/1]

Pennant, T., 1786. *A Tour in Wales*. 1991 edition. Wrexham: Bridge Books.

Philpott, R. (ed.), 2015. *The pottery and clay tobacco pipe industries of Rainford, St Helens. New research.* Liverpool: Merseyside Archaeological Society.

Philpot, S., 1978. *A study of some pottery from Hancock's Pottery, Buckley, Clwyd* Unpublished BA dissertation, University of Lancaster. [Site 14: *Buckley Archive* NMGM, III, 51, 3/3]

Pritchard, T. W., 2006. *The Making of Buckley and District*. Wrexham: Bridge Books.

Roberts, D., 1999. *The Old Villages of Denbighshire and Flintshire*. Llanrwst: Gwasg Carreg Gwalch.

Rowe, S. and Stewart, L., 2014. *Rainford roots: the archaeology of a village*. Liverpool: National Museums Liverpool and Merseyside Archaeological Society.

Rutter, J., 1977. *Buckley, Clwyd, Site 11 SJ 2767 646*. Unpublished Extra-mural Certificate in Archaeology dissertation, University of Liverpool. [Site 11: *Buckley Archive* NMGM, I, 42, 9/1]

Smith, B., and George, T. N., 1961. *British Regional Geology: North Wales*. London: HMSO.

Spavold, J. and Brown, S., 2005. *Ticknall pots and potters*. Ashbourne: Landmark Publishing Ltd.

Speakman, J., n.d./a. *Pinfold Lane, Buckley, Clwyd 1972/3*. Unpublished. [Site 2: Referred to in Knight 2001]

Speakman, J. n.d./b. *Pinfold Lane, Buckley, Clwyd (AS 31) 1984*. Unpublished. Flintshire Record Office, Hawarden, MSS NT/963. [Site 2: Finds analysis sheets 1988: *Buckley Archive* NMGM, II, 49, 7/1-12]

Thomas, C., 1985. Land Surveyors in Wales, 1750-1850: the Matthews Family. *Bulletin Board Celtic Studies* 32: 216-232.

Tyler, S., 1983. *Buckley pottery: the craft and history of the Buckley potters from the 1300s to the 1940s*. Llandudno: Mostyn Art Gallery.

Warner, R., 1813. *A Second Walk Through Wales by the Revd Richard Warner of Bath in August and September 1798*. 4th edition. Bath.

Watson, S. and Culshaw, V., 2015. *Price's Pottery, Buckley, Flintshire: Archaeological Investigations 2015*. Unpublished. CPAT Report No. 1366.

Wedd, C. B. and King, W. B. R. 1924. The geology of the country around Flint, Hawarden and Caergwrle, *Memoirs of the Geological Survey. England and Wales*. London: HMSO.

Weetman, M., 1986. *Cheapside, Ewloe Green. Report of trial excavation 30 June-11 July 1986*. Unpublished. Clwyd-Powys Archaeological Trust.

White, H., 2012. The problem of provenancing English post-medieval slipwares: a chemical and petrographic approach, *Post-Medieval Archaeology* 46-1: 56-69.

Cartographic sources

1720-1   A new map of the counties of Denbigh and Flint by William Williams. *National Library of Wales*

1733   Plan of Sir John Glynne's lordship of Hawarden. *Flintshire Record Office, HA/599*

1757 (circa) Lordship of Ewloe in parish of Hawarden belonging to Robert Davies, esq. *Flintshire Record Office, GW/651 & 652*

1779–1781   Surveys of the Gwysaney Estate belonging to John Davies, esq by Edward and John Matthews. Map XI of Ewloe Estate. Map XII of the lordship of Ewloe. *Flintshire Record Office, GW/671 & 673*

1792   Manor of Ewloe with the cottages and encroachment thereon in the parish of Hawarden (tracing). *Flintshire Record Office, GW/675*

Early 19th century   Part of Buckley Mountain. *Flintshire Record Office,* D/GW/751

1800 (circa) Hawarden area. *Flintshire Record Office,* D/DM/110

1801 (circa)   Allotments on Buckley Mountain in the townships of Gwasaney and Mold, belonging to Mrs Puleston. *Flintshire Record Office,* D/GW/681

1814   Encroachments in area of Ewloe. *Flintshire Record Office,* GW/675/B555

1815   Tracing of the Townships of Bannel, Pentrobin, Ewloe Town and Ewloe Wood from the survey of Hawarden in 1815. *Flintshire Record Office,* D/DM/809/82 (D/BJ/346)

1831   Plan of Brickworks on Buckley Mountain. *Flintshire Record Office,* D/GW/709

1834   Ordnance Survey surveyors' drawing No. 341

1839   Tithe map for Mold (Argoed township) (Apportionment of 1837)

1839   Tithe map for Mold (Bistre township) (Apportionment of 1837)

1841   Tithe map Hawarden (Apportionment of 1839)

1845   Drainage plan for land north of Buckley Mountain belonging to Philip Davies. *Flintshire Record Office,* D/GW/756

1857 (circa)   Ewloe estate in the parish of Hawarden belonging to P Davies Cooke esq *Flintshire Record Office* D/GW/752

1860 (circa)   Part of Buckley Estate (tracing). *Flintshire Record Office,* D/GW/748

1860 (circa)   Tracing of part of Buckley Estate. *Flintshire Record Office,* D/GW/749

1860 (circa)   Plan of land belonging to Philip Davies Cooke Esq. in the County of Flint. *Flintshire Record Office,* D/GWI751

1863   Portion of common on Buckley Mountain, parish of Hawarden. *Flintshire Record Office,* D/GW/724

Pre-1870   Tracing of part of Buckley Estate. *Flintshire Record Office,* D/GW/742

1870   Ordnance Survey 1st edition 1:2500, Flintshire 14.03

1871   Ordnance Survey 1st edition 1:2500, Flintshire 10.14

1872   Ordnance Survey 1st edition 1:2500, Flintshire 14.10

1874   Ordnance Survey 1st edition 1:2500, Flintshire 14.01

1875   Ordnance Survey 1st edition 1:2500, Flintshire 14.06

1884   Ordnance Survey 1st edition 1:2500, Flintshire 14.05

1899   Ordnance Survey 2nd edition 1:2500, Flintshire 10.14, 14.01, 14.03, 14.05, 14.06 and 14.10

1912   Tracing of part of PBD Cooke's estate in Buckley, revised up to 1912. *Flintshire Record Office,* D/GW/759

1912   Ordnance Survey 3rd edition 1:2500, Flintshire 10.14, 14.01, 14.03, 14.05, 14.06 and 14.10

1913   Tracing of part of Buckley Estate belonging to PBD Cooke. *Flintshire Record Office,* D/GW/760

1915   Plan of Buckley and district showing collieries, brickworks, potteries etc. *Flintshire Record Office,* D/DM/578/47

1983   Soils of England and Wales, Map sheet 2 (Wales): Soil Survey of England and Wales

1994   The Rocks of Wales, geological map of Wales: British Geological Survey

Appendix 1: Glossary

Agate ware – see joggling.

Agate-bodied ware - created by mixing two different colours of clay in such a way that they created an almost marbled surface pattern on a thrown vessel, which was then highlighted by the application of a clear glaze.

Blackware - generally covered by a dark brown to black lead glaze usually with a red under slip. Vessels from the 17th century can have a dull dark brown glaze due to over-firing, while a glossy, metallic black glaze was introduced later. Vessels range from tablewares such as cups, tankards, bowls and pitchers to large storage vessels, milk pans, and even some cooking pots.

Brown ware – A brown glazed earthenware, which was used for a range of vessel, from cups to large basins.

Blunging – a process in the preparation and purification of clay whereby it was placed in a shallow trough or pit and reduced to a liquid slip by the addition of water. The mixture was then agitated by hand or machine to separate out stones and other impurities.

Clay pan – large, shallow pond where clay slurry from blunging was left to stand to allow the clay to harden.

Clay pit – small quarry for extracting the raw clay.

Dip-pot – a medium sized vessel with a single handle often used during milking or transferring milk from one pot to another.

Fire-box – structure in base of kiln to allow fuelling.

Fire clay – a type of clay which is *refractory* and resistant to high temperatures.

Footring – a ring of clay added to the base of a vessel to lift it off the table and enable the base to be glazed.

Glaze - a thin, slip-like coating applied to pottery, the primary purposes of which include decoration and to make the piece non-porous. Basically glass. Glazes are highly variable in composition but usually comprise a mixture of ingredients that generally, but not always, mature at kiln temperatures lower than that of the pottery that it coats. Ceramic glaze raw materials generally include silica, which will be the main glass former. Various metal oxides, such as sodium, potassium and calcium, act as a flux to lower the melting temperature. In the so-called 'self-coloured' wares, the material of the glaze is derived from silicon within the clay body and is not, itself added. This applies to some Buckley 'glazes'. The flux is carried by slip to be applied, but does not necessarily contain any added silicon.

Hollow-ware – vessels designed to contain liquids or solids eg teapots, jugs, cups, bowls.

Hovel - Some kilns were surrounded by a cylindrical brick wall, the purpose of which was to protect the kiln and its workers from the weather.

Joggling - also known as 'marbling'. A variant of slipware where a vessel was coated with trailed slip, but then twisted in such a way that the trails ran across the piece and formed abstract patterns.

Kiln furniture - Refractory supports on which pottery is stacked prior to and during firing. Different types of kiln furniture, such as props, spacers and supports were used to allow a variety of wares to be fired simultaneously.

Kiln shelf – kiln shelves were usually made of fireclay to withstand the high temperatures of the kiln.

Mottled ware - most commonly occurs as a fine, buff-bodied ware covered by a yellowish lead glaze mottled with dark streaks or speckles, although coarser body fabrics were also produced. Vessels are often tankards or other table wares, but other forms were made as well.

Pan mug – a tall, large and robust bowl.

Pancheon – a wide shallow, bowl.

Pipe clay – a fine white clay used for making tobacco pipes.

Press-moulded - use of a press-mould, made from plaster of Paris or clay, into which a slab of clay is pressed to take on the form of the mould.

Refactory - a ceramic material which retains its strength at high temperatures.

Reeding – a series of ridges places around the body of a vessel. Particularly common in mottled ware tankards.

Saggar - open-topped cylinders for protecting small, more delicate pots during firing.

Sgraffito - from the Italian 'to scratch', where a layer or layers of coloured slip are applied to leather hard pottery and then scratched off selectively to create contrasting images, patterns and texture by revealing the layer(s) underneath.

Slip - clay and other materials mixed with water to create a suspension which can be used to decorate pottery.

Slipware – decorative style of pottery. Trailed slipware involving the trailing of slip to produce coloured lines or bands. This could be augmented as combed slipware by drawing a tool through the bands to create a pattern of peaks and troughs.

Stilts – small cones of clay to support smaller pots when placed inside larger pots for firing.

Stool pan – a slightly flared vessel, with a single handle. A simpler form of chamber pot.

Tankard – A tall, straight sided drinking vessel with a single handle. Buckley tankards often had distinctive fine ridges around the middle of the vessel.

Updraught kiln - The Buckley potteries appear to have used simple, circular, updraught kilns. The earlier kilns, such as those excavated at Brookhill (Site 1), had a cylindrical chamber perhaps 3m in diameter and were as tall as they were broad. Brick arches supported the floor over a single firebox and also formed flues beneath the floor to distribute the heat. The majority of the kiln structure would have been buried within a mound of earth and wasters to provide additional support for the structure as well as insulation. Only the top section of the chamber would have been visible above ground. Kilns of this type were still in use across Britain in the late 19th century, though some had by then been modified to include a domed roof by constructing a catenary arch (McGarva 2000, 90-94). A more advanced type of circular updraught kiln was the beehive design which, rather than using a surrounding mound for support, utilised iron bands to maintain the integrity of the kiln superstructure.

Wasters – pots which failed during firing.

Waste dump – collection of wasters from firing.